Sadie (standing) and Sasha.

Saving Sadie and Sasha

by

Laura S. Jones

The true story of two abandoned dogs who showed me the way home.

Published in the United States by Tidal Press.
Learn more at www.TidalPress.com.

This story is based on the author's recollection of events.

Cover photograph by the author.

ISBN: 0-9846617-2-7
ISBN-13: 978-0-9846617-2-5

DEDICATION

This book is for Sadie and Sasha. I still think about them every day. It is also for Piper and Blue, who first opened my eyes to the joys and challenges of living with "dogs with issues." And it is for all the dogs who came before them, all those who will follow, and all the ones I will never meet. If there is a heaven, it had better have *a lot* of dogs in it, or I'm not going. (Assuming of course, I even make the list in the first place, an outcome on which I might suggest *not* betting the farm.)

Everything I do is made possible by Rob. It just is, and I cannot fully explain how or why. So this book is for him, too. Finally, without Susanne Kogut or Aimee Sadler there would have been no book because there would have been no Sadie and Sasha. They are two of the most committed and talented animal welfare professionals I have ever met. This book is also for them.

TABLE OF CONTENTS

INTRODUCTION

It took one year, endless loads of laundry, crazy amounts of hot dogs, one amazing husband, one 3,400-mile road trip in the middle of winter, one canine hitchhiker, about two dozen other terrific people, a good portion of my savings and a lot of luck; but I saved Sadie and her sister Sasha. Or they saved me. I get confused. It was that kind of year. I never set out to have an adventure. Or a book. The dogs were only supposed to come home for the weekend. Two days. 48 hours. That is how an impatient optimist thinks.

They say one dog year equals seven human years, and I believe it. The year I spent with Sadie and Sasha was easily worth seven regular years, and I have the gray hairs to prove it. Still, what I did wasn't special or particularly hard. It certainly had hard moments, and it offered some pretty special memories, but I am not unique. I am just average. Anyone can do what I did, and many could do it better. Sadie and Sasha are not unique either. They are in every shelter everywhere. Go see, and fall in love for yourself.

But before we get fully into this story, there are some things you should know. This is not a dog-training book. Nor is it a book about how pit bulls make the greatest pets. Many times they do – and for me they do - but sometimes and for some people, they don't. It depends on the dog. As the folks at Animal Farm Foundation preach, "all dogs are individuals." A dog's behavior is not determined by his or her looks, just as with people. (Animal Farm Foundation is a wonderful organization whose mission is to "secure equal treatment and opportunity for "pit bull" type dogs. They helped enormously with Sadie and Sasha's journey.)

No, this is a book about what it means to provide a foster – or temporary - home for a dog in need and how the shortest chapters of our lives can sometimes have the biggest impact. It is about what it was like to take the time to really look at a couple of dogs who looked back and ended up taking me on the biggest roller coaster ride of my life. You see, I learned that looking at a dog is like listening to a person, *only better.* If you look long enough and carefully enough at a dog, you will see who the dog is, you will see into every corner of her being, into her mind, her heart and her soul. On the other hand, some people can tell you a thousand stories and you will never know a single true thing about them. Or yourself.

This is a book about loving dogs and making a gradually larger space in your life for the ones who really need you. It is also about finishing what you start. And finally, with apologies to Charles Dickens, this book is also a "Tale of Two Shelters." They are the Charlottesville Albemarle SPCA or CASPCA in Virginia (which gave Sadie and Sasha their first chance) and Longmont Humane Society in Colorado (which gave them their second). These two shelters may differ in their approach at times, but they share the same goal: to find loving homes for as many animals as possible.

I wrote this book mostly because I think the story is happy and sad and funny and universal. I also wrote it because I needed to make a memorial to Sadie and Sasha and to all the people who helped them. Finally, I wanted to provide some inspiration and courage for anyone curious about how to help dogs in shelters. Just go, open the door and walk in. Shelters are not bad, scary places and shelter dogs are not bad, scary dogs. They just aren't. You don't need the "clean slate" of a puppy to find joy with an animal. We don't insist on only having relationships with people we knew from the age of eight weeks, right? We all have baggage, and dogs carry theirs more gracefully than most people I know.

Even now, looking at the photo of Sadie and Sasha on the cover of this book (something I do *waaayyyy* too often for it to be a remotely healthy activity), my knees go weak and I get a lump in my throat. Yes, you are reading a book written by a dopey, sappy, crybaby. Sorry. Stop now if that bothers you.

My husband Rob and I went on such a journey with these two sweet, terrified dogs that their absence has left a permanent hole in our house. A necessary hole, but still a hole. That is the nature of fostering: you love, they leave. Sadie and Sasha were so intensely here in our house, though, that in some way I believe they shed part of themselves. (And I don't just mean the dog hair and pee stains and chewed up rocking chair which I will never, ever get rid of.)

In the end, I believe we are most human when we interact outside our species. I also believe – no, I know - that loving difficult dogs taught me better how to love people and myself. It hurts sometimes, but that's okay. Call it what you will: magic, the universe, collective unconscious, God. Maybe it is something inside us that sleeps through most of our lives but wakes up a few times to give us these flashes of intense meaning and connectedness. But "it" showed up in the form of Sadie and Sasha, and I am grateful.

I miss the way Sadie wagged her tail in a circle. Always clockwise. I miss the way Sasha beat her front paws on the ground to show her joy. I miss the way the two of them would charge down the narrow hall in the morning, a reckless mass of legs and tails and heads careening into each other and the walls. They looked like they would fly apart with the force of their happiness.

This quote from *The Outermost House* written by naturalist Henry Beston about a year he spent living on the Cape Cod coast, sums it up perfectly:

> Remote from universal nature, and living by complicated artifice, man in civilization surveys the creature through the glass of his knowledge and sees there a feather magnified and the whole image in distortion. We patronize them for their incompleteness, for their tragic fate of having taken form so far below ourselves. And therein we err, and greatly err. For the animal shall not be measured by man. In a world older and more complete than ours, they move finished and complete, given with extensions of the senses we have lost or never attained, living by voices we shall never hear. They are not brethren, they are not underlings; they are other nations, caught with ourselves in the net of life and time, fellow prisoners of the splendor and travail of the earth.

For a wonderful time the girls and I were "fellow prisoners of the splendor and travail of the earth." Here is what happened.

PART ONE: The Tilt-a-Whirl Starts Up

Chapter 1 – Buckle Your Seatbelt and Hold On

When I walked into the lobby of the Charlottesville-Albemarle SPCA in central Virginia a little after 4pm on that Friday in April, 2011, Ashley, the Front Desk Manager, spotted me before the door could swing shut.

"They're upstairs in Michelle's office," she said, grinning at me over the long line at the front desk. Michelle was the Clinic Manager and a fellow lover of shy dogs.

"Okay, thanks," I said, practically vibrating with anticipation.

It was a gorgeous afternoon, and I was going to meet my foster dogs for the first time. *My* foster dogs! I felt so grown up. I had always thought one day I would do this with children, so in a way this was a step toward that potential goal. At least that was what I told myself to justify the fact that I wanted more dogs in the house. I am very susceptible to spring fever, and this spring, I had a fever for dogs. I was nervous, though. It is one thing to adopt a happy, healthy dog eager to go home with you; it's another thing to be in loco parentis for dogs who need help. You're just borrowing them, and you better not screw them up. It reminded me of the time I drove my boss' tricked-out Acura to a meeting when my car, a beat-up Ford Taurus on its third transmission, was in the shop. Multiplied by like a million.

My last day as an employee of the shelter was about a year earlier. I was the Volunteer Coordinator, and in that capacity, one of my jobs was to train new volunteers to be dog walkers. I spent a lot of time with the dogs so I could introduce new folks to the diversity of canine personalities that they would face. I also filled in as needed with any and every other task; that is the nature of non-profits in general and shelters specifically. Everybody has to be able to do everything, up to and including holding dogs when they are euthanized. I know it's overly dramatic and probably insulting to our men and women in uniform, but when people asked me why I left, I often equated working at a shelter with doing a tour of duty in Iraq. It was hard work – important - but very hard. I felt like I had had a mild case of post-traumatic stress syndrome when I left. In the months that followed, I had dabbled with walking dogs and helped out by writing articles and volunteering for the occasional adoption event, but now I was finally healthy enough for more.

But back to Sadie and Sasha. I had already agreed to take them home for the weekend sight unseen. I knew plenty about their type, though: neglected pit bulls with a deep fear of people. Not only did I love this particular flavor of abandoned animal, I felt a kinship with them. People often confused and disappointed me, too. But dogs, dogs rarely did. Although I had no way of knowing it then, these girls were going to test that belief in ways I could have never imagined.

With two new leashes in my hands, I trotted past the lobby cats, through the glass double doors and down the hall to the stairs. I had gotten the leashes from the pet store a block from the shelter. The day before, I had spent a ridiculously long time selecting them. They needed to be six feet long, with comfortable handles and a strong clasp. I had walked enough shelter dogs to know what equipment is best. But the design was important too, because it sends a message. I went with colorful peace signs on one leash and a gray paisley on the other. I had plenty of leashes at home, but I couldn't see starting this new adventure without purchasing something just for them.

Michelle's office door was open when I got there, but I saw no dogs.

"Where are they?" I asked, feeling an odd sense of panic. Ashley had told me they were there, so they couldn't be euthanized already. But what if they had bitten someone? Fearful dogs can bite – it is understandable but not allowed in the shelter environment.

"Under here," Michelle said, pointing to the top of her desk and scooting her chair back. I came around to look. Pressed against the back panel of her desk were two dogs trying their best to be invisible. One had a dark coat with a brush of white on her face and a white chest. The other was a patchwork of brown and white, like a cow, but had a mostly white face. Sasha, the one with the white face and was huddled behind her sister, Sadie. Both were as tense as a bow about to release an arrow, and they clearly had been in that state for a long time.

Their heads were pointed away from me, but I could see each dog's right eye and those eyes were big as saucers. A dog's eyes can reveal all you need to know about her emotional state, even if you can only see one. Some dog behaviorists call that saucer-eyed look "whale eye," when you can see a big crescent shaped slice of the white of the eye, and it is not good.

Sasha's intake photo in her kennel.

Sadie's intake photo on a chair in the lobby. She jumped on the first thing she could, looking for an escape.

"Do NOT come any closer," those whale eyes said. "Really."

It was a big, flashing warning sign that I had to ignore, or I would never get these girls out from under the desk, into my car, and home to meet their temporary canine siblings. It was not so much me I was worried about – it was them. If they bit me, they would have to be put down. Killed in order to protect the public. Shelters would not be in business long if they sent biting pit bulls – or anything big and bite-y – out into the world. (Cats and Chihuahuas were allowed to bite, because sometimes, that is the essence of who they are. They are also small with small teeth.)

Sasha's eye kept talking, though, oblivious to the trouble it could make for her. "If you even think about coming under here, I'll bite you. So, um stay away. Okay? I'm not really a biter, I just have to act tough, because well, my life was tough, and this is so confusing, and…um. Just back off." It was a chatty eyeball. Sadie's eye conveyed a different message: "I'm not here. You're not there. Mmmmmm. I'm in my happy place. Happy, la, la, la, la. Not here. Okay?"

Sadie and Sasha were in this state because they had spent the first nine months of their lives locked in a backyard cage, the unwanted leftovers from a litter whose siblings had long been sold. They were terribly thin when a neighbor brought them into the shelter. They weren't fighting dogs - no, nothing dramatic like that. Like too many dogs, they were just ignored.

It didn't take long to realize that what those eyes *wanted* to say was "Please help me," but they didn't speak our language. It also wasn't long before their fear *of* me turned into a fear of *losing* me.

But I am getting ahead of myself. First, I had to drag the girls out from under the desk. It certainly helps to be both somewhat limber and dressed in clothes you are not too fond of when you attempt dog rescue. (Although I've always disliked the term "rescue dog." As in when someone introduces his or her pet with: "She's a rescue!" It makes me want to ask, "So, did you hang out of a helicopter and grab her collar and pull her battered body out a raging river just before she plunged over a waterfall to certain death on the rocks below?" No, you went to a shelter and picked out the dog that jumped up on his kennel door and wagged his tail at you. It is just as heroic an act, but can we just call them shelter dogs and not rescue dogs? Unless, of course, you did the helicopter thing. In which case, my apologies.)

I took a breath and reached under and despite the eye chatter, there was no biting. I clipped my new leashes onto their collars and dragged them out. Victory! (Ideally, I wouldn't have dragged them out – it's just not a nice way to be introduced – but I didn't have time to gain their trust before getting them home.) I hadn't decided on how to get them from the second floor to the outside, though. It would have probably been easier to lower them out of a window, but I decided on the elevator. Believe it or not, stairs are sometimes harder to negotiate with a shy dog. Somehow the elevator plan worked and we got out of the shelter before they realized what was happening.

By the time we got to the car, though, they had become convinced they were going to be fed to dragons. After twenty minutes of sweaty farce under gathering clouds, I got them loaded into my car. The process was complicated by the fact that as soon as

I'd get one in, she'd jump out as I tried to grab the other one. Eventually, Sasha mistimed a jump and I was able to slide the rear passenger door shut. They made it look much easier than this on old episodes of *Wild Kingdom*. Then again, I think they had tranquilizer guns.

With a deep breath, I started the car and headed for home.

"I trust you," my husband Rob had said when I asked if he wanted to meet the girls before I brought them home. I was proud of that trust and a little afraid I was abusing it. This was going to wreck our weekend. But if I did anything right way back in my twenties, it was marrying this man.

How Sadie and Sasha spent their first days.
Backs to the wall and watching.

Chapter 2 – "We're Not in Kansas Anymore"

As I was driving Sadie and Sasha the three miles to our house, I began to smell pee. Okay, no big deal, I thought; pee is easy to clean up and it's not like you could eat off the floor of my car anyway. I lowered my driver's side window to let some fresh air in. Pee from a scared dog who had been eating god-knows-what smells much worse than pee from a well-fed and emotionally healthy dog. Go figure, right?

Two faces suddenly appeared in the rearview mirror, expressions filled with a mixture of hope and adrenaline. You know the look; you've seen it on the third-string kicker in a high school football game with the game on the line. Or on Dorothy when she landed in Oz after the tornado. Sadie and Sasha had felt the breeze from my open window and decided escape might be possible. I did not put the leap past them and quickly mashed the button to raise the window. Their heads retreated in disappointment and disgust. A minute later, I pulled into my driveway and turned off the car. I looked back to find my two 35-pound foster dogs trying to wedge themselves headfirst under the passenger seat. I understood their thinking. You'd have to be a moron not to, it was that clear: "If I can't see you, you can't see me, and if you can't see me, you can't hurt me." A tornado had lifted them out of the world they knew, and dropped them into one they knew nothing about, one they assumed would be far, far worse. And why not? That was the trajectory their lives had followed so far.

I took a deep breath and tried to plan a strategy. Getting them into the car was hard enough, so how was I going to get them out?

Just then, Rob opened our front door and was walking down the stairs smiling. Thank goodness he was home. The odds were looking better. With one person per dog, we had a chance of getting them safely into the backyard - I wasn't even thinking about the house yet. I was completely afraid that I was in over my head, but I smiled back as if all was going as planned. "Fake it 'til you make it" was becoming the motto for this day. (And indeed for the coming year, but if I had known that, I might not have gotten into this wonderful mess.)

I got out and walked around the car and opened the rear passenger door, simultaneously grabbing both leashes in case they were thinking about bolting.

"They're cute," he said, still smiling and peering inside at their backs.

"They're adorable," I agreed. One of the many things it helps to have in common with your husband is an affinity for the same kind of dog. Although my childhood dog was a Standard Poodle and he started with a Basset Hound and then had a Bulldog as a teenager, we had come to be unabashed fans of the pit bull mutt, particularly ones with white faces like Sasha. It is all Piper's fault. Piper is our home's "queen bee," a pit bull mutt who wormed her way into our hearts with her sheer beauty, desperately neurotic needs, joyful play, and pushy nose.

"What should I do?" Rob asked.

I had no idea. I hadn't planned this far. For some reason, I often find myself in these kinds of situations. Look before you leap? So boring.

It had taken forever and some luck to get them into the car; I really hadn't figured out how to get them out. In the shelter's parking lot, each time I got one in, she jumped out as I picked up the other one. Somehow I broke the cycle, but I wasn't sure how to reverse it, and my back was exhausted. "Here, take Sadie's leash," I said. For whatever reason, I had decided that Sadie was less likely to bite.

"Should I just grab her?" Rob was not scared at all. I don't think he realized the depths of their issues, thank goodness.

"No, no, no. Wait. Let me pull her out, just hold on to her leash." If anyone was going to get bitten, it had to be me. This was my responsibility; I had brought them into the family.

So with my left hand clamped on Sasha's leash, I wrapped my arms around Sadie's back half and pulled her out. She felt like a sack of potatoes. Lifeless and unwieldy. I put her on the ground and she froze. Rob tried to cajole her up the stairs, but she would have none of it. The upside was that Sasha pulled her head out from under the seat with a "Where's my sister?" look. I dove for her and scooped her out of the car, closing the door so no one could jump back in.

There was a tension in the air I had never felt, a crackling anticipation. There was no time to congratulate ourselves. Sadie bolted up the hill of our front yard. Sasha followed on her heels, and since Rob and I were attached by the leashes, we went along for the ride, trying to make our legs move fast enough to keep from falling over and being dragged. I fumbled open the gate to the back yard, and both girls froze again, paralyzed by what we would later understand to be a serious fear of thresholds. You could see them trying to decide what was scarier, us or the gate. They decided simultaneously, probably thanks to a telepathy developed from spending their whole lives in a tiny space with just each other, and ran in. We dropped their leashes before our arms got yanked off and closed the gate. (Susanne Kogut, the Executive Director of the CASPCA at the time and foster parent for many near-feral dogs, had warned me to leave a frightened dog's leash attached to her collar so you can catch her without having to reach for her head and scare her even more or risk getting bitten.)

It wasn't the homecoming scene I imagined when I decided to become a foster parent. I felt more like I was taking a pair of hostages into custody. Piper's barking didn't help. She always barked when we came home, but this was different. This was the "Whoa, new dogs? No one asked me!" bark. Piper doesn't particularly like other dogs. That was another complication, but one I figured we could work around. It took her many weeks to accept our other dog Blue after we brought him home, and Blue was a pretty easy-going dog. They still live in a kind of "peace through strength" way, but they also sleep together when it is cold. And Blue cleans Piper's ears when she asks him. It is pretty cute.

We left the girls alone in the backyard to catch their breath before throwing them any more curveballs and went inside to calm Piper. Blue, on the other hand, was so excited to go and see the new additions. He was wagging his tail and stomping his feet and whining. Every fiber of his being was shouting: "These are the best new toys ever! Is it Christmas? It must be Christmas! Thank you, thank you, thank you! Can I go play with them now, please, please, please?" He punctuated his requests with glances at the back door in case we had forgotten how to access the yard (and needed reminding.)

Maybe it was because I was exhausted, but we made the incautious decision to let Blue and Piper into the backyard about ten minutes later. Four pit bulls in one small yard. There are all sorts of rules for introductions that I knew I completely ignored. I just ripped off the Band-Aid and figured they could sort it out.

Well, Sasha and Piper took a bit of an instant dislike to each other - probably because in many ways, they are exactly the same. Blue stuck up for his sister, which was so sweet but not really helpful. More specifically, Piper was overwhelmed and lunged at Sasha who was still six feet away. Sasha got the message and although she bared her teeth and fake-lunged, she kept her distance. Blue decided he had to back up his sister anyway, so he went after Sasha. I yelled, Sasha ran, and Blue stopped and looked at me with confusion. "I was only getting my sister's back. She seemed upset with these new things. Of course, I thought they were completely wonderful, but I will always stick up for my sister." Blue can say a lot with one look. I encouraged Piper and Blue to go back inside and calm down. Bad Laura. I knew better, but knowing and doing, as I learned again and again on this journey, are two very different things.

So we had a temporary mess - not quite a dog fight, but close. Undoubtedly, Piper and Blue sensed my tension and figured the newcomers must be the source of it. Then there was the bolt of lightning. Thunder, as is its habit, immediately followed. Then came the sheets of rain and hail. Seriously, hail. We bolted for the door and thought the girls would be right behind. Sure, they were afraid of us, but we're less scary than the storm of the century, right? Nope, the girls had disappeared. Of course, I realized, nature, in all its fury and glory, was perfectly normal to them. People were not.

I was frantic. I had lost them. We had a fully fenced yard, but they could have jumped the fence. It would have been a huge effort for they were not big or strong dogs, but fear does pump a lot of adrenaline through a body. I searched all over. I ran into the front yard, down the street. I went back into the yard to every corner. Drenched and panicked, I kept going over the same ground. Rob looked as well. Nothing. They were gone and would probably be dead soon, hit by a car. I had failed them already, before I could show them how much I loved them. I cried huge, gulping sobs that were lost in the rain.

Something told me to get over myself and not give up, and on my third pass over the far right corner of our yard, I found them. They were huddled next to each other, their bodies pressed against each other and our dilapidated shed. They quaked with terror once they saw me. Really, they must have felt they had been dropped onto the moon. I was sympathetic, and I probably should have left them alone, but my gut said "get them in the house where it is safe." Dogs are adaptable, and they will recover from this, I told myself. Whatever "this" is. I grabbed for a leash without even knowing who was attached to it, and both dogs bolted away from me but toward the house. Progress! I thought. I followed them, feeling like a Border Collie herding sheep, but they veered off at the last minute. Frustrated and exhausted, I went inside to squeeze some water out of my clothes and prepare to try again. They were in the yard at least.

Rob saw how much I needed them inside, so he went out into the storm and grabbed Sasha. I don't know how - I didn't see it - but he is a pretty athletic guy. I had a towel ready and he handed her to me in the laundry room, which is tiny for one person, much less one person and a terrified, wet dog. I tried to dry her without scaring her more. Undoubtedly she thought the towel was a newfangled suffocation device. After I got some of the water and dirt off of her, I opened the door to let her out and she bolted down the hall to the guest room, the point farthest away from me. Rob quickly presented me with a sopping Sadie. She accepted only a single pass of the towel before panicking, bucking like a wild horse. I let her out and she made a beeline for her sister under the guest bed. It was like they had radar for each other.

Their crate was already set up in that guest room, with a soft bed and water bowls so after making sure they were unhurt, I closed the guest room door. I needed a minute to regroup anyway. We fed our dogs, and then I took two bowls of food into the guest room. It was an insufficiently exciting bribe - although they both squirmed under the bed as if they wanted to come out, but just couldn't summon the courage. They had to be starving so I left the bowls on the floor and went to change my clothes. I soon heard their nails gently tapping on the floor, as they tip-toed out to eat.

I was so relieved that I almost cried again. Any dog who eats is not that terrified. It wasn't supposed to be this hard, though. I wasn't sure it was entirely the storm's fault either. Why did I think I could do this? I felt the same sense of imposter syndrome I did when I was a young lawyer going into a courtroom. The fancy suit and graduation-present-briefcase and weeks of preparation did nothing to ease a feeling of imminent disaster. "That's okay," I told myself, "It's just for the weekend. Plus, they have to be better tomorrow. They just do." And they were better, after I realized the total world-changing power of bribes.

Chapter 3 – A Bit of Background

We had intended to foster just one dog, Dutch, a long-legged brindle-coated pit bull mix who had been in the shelter a long time, nearly a year. He was a little shy, too, and often seemed just sort of lost. Rob had already met Dutch and had a soft spot for him, too. This young dog had good days and bad days and was suffering from an occasional limp that probably needed exercise to improve. He was overlooked by potential adopters because he wasn't an eager people-pleaser. He reacted to the chaos of the shelter environment by withdrawing, and it is hard if not impossible to charm people that way. I figured he could use some time romping in a yard as well as a few naps on the couch. And some extra food - he was a skinny fellow. But he was adopted the day before I was going to bring him home. It was a much better outcome for Dutch, and, of course, it freed me up to take Sadie and Sasha, but I was still a little sad.

Dutch got to enjoy (which may not be exactly the right word) such a long path to adoption because the Charlottesville-Albemarle SPCA is a "No-Kill" shelter meaning that we did not euthanize animals solely because we didn't have the space or resources to take care of them. We found space, primarily through fostering or putting dogs in employee offices, and we made resources by pleading to the community for money. (Social media makes this easier and faster now.) Animals were only euthanized if they were too sick or too dangerous to be adopted into the community. (The word "dangerous" can be defined many different ways and reasonable minds can differ, a fact that comes into play in this story in a big way.) From 2009-2014 when I was involved with the CASPCA as a staff person and volunteer, we saved, on average, more than 90 percent of the animals that came through our doors, and we had to take every stray or abandoned animal because we were also the city and county pound. Over the course of each of those years, the CASPCA provided shelter for about 4,000 dogs and cats and small animals (hamsters and rabbits and guinea pigs.) At any given time, we may have had 300 animals in our care, with about 200 of those available for adoption. The ones not available for adoption were waiting for their owners to claim them, or undergoing behavior training programs, or receiving medical attention from the in-house veterinary clinic. So we did pretty good most of the time, but there was a limit.[1]

Generally, dogs come into the shelter as strays, owner surrenders, or seizures from abuse and neglect cases. Rarely does the whole truth come in the doors with the dogs. But all dogs at the shelter (any shelter, probably), wherever they initially come from, fall into ten categories: Purebreds; lab mixes; fluffy dogs; little cute dogs; little biting dogs; beagles; large hounds; pit bulls; put bull mixes; and scratch-and-dent. (I'm leaving out puppies because they usually get adopted before they even realize where they are.) Scratch-and-dent could then be divided into dogs with physical

---

[1] The term "No-Kill" is becoming controversial for many good reasons. It implies that no animal is ever euthanized, which is not true. Some in the animal welfare community also argue that the policies embraced by the No-Kill movement mean animals suffer from over-crowded conditions or get placed in homes that are not properly screened. I can only write about what I know, which is that the Charlottesville-Albemarle SPCA under Susanne Kogut saved an amazing number of lives that would have otherwise been lost unnecessarily.

issues and those with emotional issues. We lovingly called the dogs with emotional issues "weirdos." Perhaps it wasn't the kindest moniker, but it was accurate. So, of the ten categories of dogs, purebreds through beagles get adopted fairly quickly. (Yes, people seem to prefer even little biting dogs to large hounds or pit bulls.)

Our volunteers and staff would separate into categories that roughly matched the last four. Emily Beichel, our vet, loved the medical scratch-and-dent cases, the injured or sick dogs. Heather, who had held every job in the shelter over the years, fell for the hounds and the weirdos. Ashley, the front desk manager, and I loved the pit bulls and pit bull mixes, especially the shy ones. No one allowed themselves to develop a crush on a Pomeranian or a Labrador mix. They didn't need us; they sold themselves quite well to potential adopters.

All ten categories of dogs undergo temperament testing to determine what type of home might work best and how they might behave in the community. You don't want to place a high-energy, nervous dog with an older adult or with a family that has young children who may not understand the dog's personal boundaries. The CASPCA, like many other shelters, has an established plan and timeline for the evaluation of a dog's behavior. At the CASPCA, all dogs had to be evaluated with a food test, handling test and stranger test, among others. Nathan Winograd, founder of No-Kill Nation, explains the need for temperament testing as follows:

> Temperament testing is a series of exercises designed to evaluate whether an animal is aggressive. Because dog behavior is highly specific to context, it is unfortunately not enough to say that a dog is friendly and of reasonably good

temperament if she comes into a shelter with her tail wagging. The flip side is also true. Because the shelter is a highly stressful, unnatural, and frightening environment for a dog who has just been abandoned by a family, the fact that a dog is scared and growls at staff on intake is not enough to make a determination that the dog is unfriendly and vicious. So it is not only fair, but a good idea, for shelters to evaluate dogs to make sure they can safely be placed into loving new homes. But temperament testing has many limitations. It requires skill and training; the results greatly depend on the environment in which the test is conducted; and, because its predictive validity has not been proven, it can – and sometimes does – result in dogs being wrongly executed.

Temperament testing at the CASPCA also includes: seeing how the dog reacts when you check his teeth and handle his feet; if she likes to play with toys and if you can take a toy away from her; if he likes to be petted,; if she startles easily; if he will eat when you are standing over him; and if she growls at you when you take the food away. Another rule at the CASPCA, and many other shelters, was that any dominant breed dog had to undergo further temperament testing to determine if she could be safely adopted. Some more enlightened shelters do not distinguish based on breeds, but things move slowly in the South. And you have to play within the rules to do any good. Pit bulls, Bull Terriers, Bulldogs, Rottweilers, Dobermans, Boxers and German shepherds are all examples of dominant breed dogs. (Anything with "bull" in the name was also called a bully breed. Sometimes they were actual bullies and for the same reason people are bullies: fear and insecurity and a need to feel safe through strength. It was our job as people who cared for these dogs to convince them they didn't need to be bullies.)

So-called dominant breed dogs theoretically needed extra scrutiny because they are big, strong dogs and should they choose to do something you'd rather them not, they are hard to stop. Theoretically, if a dog adopted from a shelter injures or kills a person or another animal, the shelter would at a minimum have a public relations issue on its hands and at the most, a lawsuit. Also theoretically, the shelter's ability to help other animals may be impacted. So the handling of potentially dangerous dogs is the biggest issue at our shelter and many shelters. But potentially dangerous dogs still have big, brown, beautiful and loving eyes. It is all so complicated. So, in other words, each dog deserves to be evaluated as an individual, even if there were some pre-conceived notions that may – or may not - have a basis in fact.

This extra scrutiny included cat testing and seeing how the dog would play with other dogs. Cat testing was always entertaining. We would keep the dog on a leash and let the cat free in the lunchroom. We always selected a cat with some attitude ("cattitude") and street smarts so the test wouldn't stress her too much. The trick was to gauge the dog's interest in killing the cat. Part of the test included looking at the cat, at least for me. If the cat was relaxed, even if the dog looked a little too interested, the dog was probably not a potential cat-killer.

Dog-to-dog testing was a little trickier. Both dogs had to eventually come off the leash, which meant you would have no way of separating them if they wanted to fight. Luckily, dogs are pack animals and don't usually want to fight. We liked to set them up to succeed by testing males with females, thereby avoiding the territorial contests that can occur a little more often between dogs of the same sex. One fair assessment of pit bulls in particular is that they can be "dog-selective," or as some of us like to say, "picky about their dog friends." And they may play rough because they are so athletic. But most dogs at a shelter are craving exercise and play with their own kind since they have to be kept in kennels, usually alone, for most of every day. Usually these tests went well.

The problem with shy dogs, regardless of breed, is that they probably don't show their true temperaments in any of these tests. It's like if you are travelling in a strange country and don't know the language or customs. You'd probably be a little off your game. Shy dogs are too afraid to eat, so you don't know if they are food guarders. They are afraid of strangers and of you. It is impossible to tell how they will behave if they overcome their fear; you can't adopt out dominant breed dogs when you don't know their true personality. Or at least that was the CASPCA's position. Sometimes with shy dogs we would wait to test, but some dogs get worse as they wait. Some dogs get better, but only with a lot of staff attention. And when Sadie and Sasha came in, much of the staff already had their "project dogs." Sadie and Sasha simply couldn't be temperament-tested; if they were, they would fail. They were catatonic with fear. So, if they didn't get a foster home, they could wait, but that would mean weeks in the back kennels not available for adoption. There was a chance, too, that something bad could happen while they waited. They could escape, bite someone, or become sick.

In addition to official temperament-testing, the staff also kept notes of any concerning (or positive) behavior. According to the notes on Sadie and Sasha's first interactions with people; they did not show themselves particularly well. Here's one from Sadie's first day:

> When I approached her kennel she ran away from me and avoids me but is wagging tail. Then when I turn my back on her and go to walk away, she lunges towards the kennel door and is barking at me.

And from Sasha's second day:

> As I walked in front of Sasha's kennel she ran from the front of the kennel to the outside. Once I walked by, Sasha came from outside, approached the front of the kennel, put her front paws on it and began barking at me. When I turned around and walked up to her kennel she ran away.

Both behaviors are excellent descriptions of "fear aggression," which means exactly what it sounds like. A fearful dog will act aggressively because she is afraid of you, not because she wants to kill you. She wants you to GO AWAY. It's like one of those puffer fish puffing up when a shark swims by. With fear aggression, the plan is to convince the dog that the thing he fears, in this case people, only means great things for him. This is hard to do in a shelter where you can't control all the interactions the dogs have with people. Through fostering, though, shy or troubled dogs can get a test drive in a safe place with controlled interactions. We can see how they behave when they lose their fear. But with Sadie and Sasha, it was still a huge gamble, a huge responsibility. I had to keep them safe, keep my dog and cats safe, and keep the community safe.

Something told me they wouldn't hurt a soul, but I had been wrong before. I still remember the dogs I sat with when they were euthanized. I will never forget them. It is a terrible privilege to be with an animal when he or she dies – that is how I trained myself to think. It was my job to give them love until the last moment, but it is also something you cannot do too often without hardening your heart beyond repair.

So the purpose of all this background is to explain that Sadie and Sasha were not about to be euthanized, but they weren't on a good path. It was my job to see who they really were and see if I could calm their fear enough for them to let the world see what I hoped I could see in their souls.

Before I get back to Sadie and Sasha, I must define the most important term of all: pit bull. "Pit bull" is a garbage term. It is slang. It describes a mutt. Pit bulls usually bear some physical resemblance to American Staffordshire Terriers or American Pit Bull Terriers or Bull Terriers or American Bulldogs, but they have a vastly more diverse DNA profile than these "pure bred" dogs. Animal Farm Foundation has done excellent research on what, if anything, it means for a dog to be called a pit bull, other than they are vastly more likely to be the victims of breed discrimination laws. But, I would argue that the dogs we commonly see as "pit bulls" have the following similarities: they have strong bodies, a whip like tail, wide heads and wide eyes. They have short hair. They smile, and they'd rather be with you than anywhere else in the world. They love couches and usually hate water. They will play fetch like it is their duty. They will lick your face whether you have food on it or not. They want to make you happy more than they want to make themselves happy, at least most of the time. They can find some dogs hard to get along with. They can be bullied by cats. They are dogs for people who want to feel needed. They are beautiful and they are strong, but they are not always popular. They are individuals, too. And most importantly of all in this far too busy world, they are excellent at napping with you on the couch. (Okay, so maybe this is partly a book about how pit bulls make the best pets.....)

Saving Sadie and Sasha

Chapter 4 – My Mother Always Said

My mother always said that the most basic human need is to be understood. Assuming she meant after you have food, water and shelter, I think she may be right. I also think her insight applies to dogs as well. To understand someone else, and to in turn be understood, is a gift like none other. It is the definition of intimacy itself. Arguably, my mother believed this so wholeheartedly because she was never very well understood herself. And I think she was never very well understood because she didn't let people in. She didn't trust them to see inside and still like her. Thanks to force of habit, she is still afraid to put her whole self out there, even at 80, an age at which I hope to God I don't care what people think anymore.

At the beginning of our time together, Sadie and Sasha were similarly afraid. They probably didn't even know who they were since they never had really engaged with the world. They didn't understand themselves. But I made a few guesses about them after our crazy evening, and I was right. Not because I am such a genius but because dogs usually are needy, loving, responsive creatures. If you respond to their posturing and become afraid of them, they will confirm your fear. Like people, or indeed any intuitive creature, they are who you think they are, to a large degree.

Dogs speak not with words, but with their bodies: ears, tail, eyes, mouth, fur and muscles. Bodies don't lie as easily as words do. It takes some time to learn and understand a dog's body and its language, but it is worth it. With a dog you don't know well, you have to scan its body frequently as you make friends. Sadie and

Sasha on alert, tail tucked and body tense.

Sasha made this easy. Like the stereotypical American tourists in Europe, they shouted in order to be understood - only they shouted with their bodies. They cowered with tucked tails and whale eyes, and their ears were pressed flat against their heads. Oh, and they quivered. I had to teach them to trust me, which means I had to let them understand me, too.

I couldn't let them see my incompetence, my own crazy fears, my tiredness, my exasperation, anything. They could only be allowed to sense calm confidence. To me, projecting calm confidence was harder than backing up a trailer on a hill. But I was going to try. I had to. Interestingly enough, the more I faked it for them, the more confident I felt.

Rob and I had planned to keep Sadie and Sasha in the guest room until Piper, our queen bee, understood they were not a threat and we were not replacing her. (Why have a second bedroom if you don't use it?) It was not the ideal situation, but we needed a dog fight like we needed a hole in the head. Plus, no one in the sheltering world really looks for "ideal". We look for good enough. So, with the dogs separated – Piper and Blue with us and Sadie and Sasha in the guest room – the first night was still not a quiet one. For dogs who were so scared of us, Sadie and Sasha desperately wanted to be with us. Whether it was curiosity about things going on that they couldn't see, or nascent loneliness, or some sense that we were their saviors (I pick that one), they were restless. Sasha whined almost from the moment we said goodnight. After a couple of hours of pretending I didn't hear it, I went in there to sleep with them. They seemed happy to see me, though, so I called it progress. I also let them out of the crate to "sleep" with me. Now, there are all sorts of theories on how to soothe a crying dog or baby. But I couldn't remember them because it was freaking 2:30 in the morning, and I was too old to be awake at this hour. There is a reason we are designed to have babies or go to outrageous parties in our twenties, and it is because at that age we can function at 2:30 in the morning. At 46, not so much.

So in or out of the crate, sleeping was not on the agenda. Peeing was (I just left the accidents til morning) and so was hiding in the corner and chewing things. These were all perfectly normal behaviors for essentially feral dogs, but not super appealing in the MIDDLE OF THE NIGHT. I was losing touch with my lofty ideals. Coffee and daylight would help, I figured. Or I hoped. I heard Rob get up around 5:30am, and I stood up to open the door. Well, that activity sent the girls diving for cover back in their crate. Apparently

I was cool only so long as I was horizontal. So I closed the door and headed for the kitchen thinking I'd just have some coffee before I did anything else. Little did I know that rising at 5:30 in the morning would become our new normal.

After letting Piper and Blue out to reclaim their back yard, we tried to wake up enough to face another round of dog introductions. I went to check on the girls and they bounded out to see me, so I opened the door to invite them into the hallway. "No, the hallway is scary," their bodies said as they shied back into the corner. "Okay, maybe later," I said out loud and turned my back to leave. Well, that brought them dancing back out, so I turned around and they shrunk back as if I were going to hit them. Poor things. Their tails were wagging as if they wanted so much to follow me. It would have been comical if it weren't so frustrating. (Well, it was kind of funny.) "And it is the first day," I told myself. "Breathe. Don't be so impatient; they have a lot of unlearning to do."

After a few more back-and-forths, the girls finally followed me down the hall out of basic puppy curiosity. Neither wanted to lead, though, so they would get stuck in the narrow hallway. (Let me explain our house layout: it is a ranch with a full basement. But no one was going in the basement until much later. That will be an adventure unto itself. Bedrooms are at one end, kitchen and living room and finally office at the other. There is a long-ish narrow hallway – we named it the "trip zone" – between the bedrooms at one end of the house and my office at the other.) If I turned around on that inaugural trip down the hallway, they would freeze. Seriously, it was like something out of a cartoon. When they finally

An early breakfast. Sadie and Sasha are not actually sure they are getting a bowl yet. They would like to leave, but being scared of doorways made that difficult.

made it into the kitchen after their two-steps-forward-one-step-back dance, breakfast cheered everyone up. You could see their delight.

"Food again? After dinner last night? Wow!"

They showed their happiness by literally dancing a jig. It was pretty darn cute. It is so hard in life to make anyone *that* happy, especially just with food. Most of us get immune to the joys of breakfast after a while, unless it's blueberry pancakes with maple syrup.

Feeding four dogs is tricky, though. We didn't have the counter space in our small kitchen for four dog bowls, so two sat on the stove top. We filled everyone's bowl, and then I walked back to the guest room to feed the girls in there. They quite liked their food and managed to bunny hop on two legs almost the whole way trying to get it out of my hands. They showed no food aggression with each other, which was a big relief. Although we did not push our luck by trying to feed them in the same room as our dogs. Piper and Blue are good with each other, too, and we can handle them all we want while they are eating, but there was no need to set anyone up to fail. We had introduced enough newness in the past twelve hours. One new dog is one thing, but two new dogs really change the dynamic. (I learned that lesson in spades later when I thought everyone was comfortable with each other. I foolishly gave all the dogs rawhide bones in the backyard. Rawhides are more special than dinner because they are doled out less frequently, and thus are a much more precious resource. Sasha and Blue quickly and loudly decided they wanted each other's. But I am getting ahead of myself. All is good now.)

I stayed with the girls while they ate and Rob fed Piper and Blue. Then he corralled our dogs in our bedroom and I tried to get the girls to go outside in the hopes we could get them housebroken quickly. All went pretty well until we got to the door.

"Yes! We want to go outside, but not through a scary door for god's sake! Isn't there another way? Can't you do magic, like wiggle your nose or something, or maybe you could open a window? That window doesn't look so bad!"

They were still absolutely terrified of doorways.

I was desperate to get them to pee and poop – I mentioned that I can be impatient, right? - so I heaved them outside. There are two schools of thought – well, there are probably more than two – about handling fear in a dog. One is to comfort the dog and reward small steps and the other is to help her "push" through it, in a safe and supportive way. I needed more coffee, and I needed them to pee, so I went for the "pushing through it" theory. It was traumatic but short-lived. It was neither my first nor last mistake with these girls. Once outside, they forgot the temporary trauma and were happy enough to explore. They did try to run a little which was funny since they clearly never had run before. Their muscles were underdeveloped from spending their entire life in a cage. They did keep looking at me, as if wondering why I needed to be there. It reminded me of the scene in *Finding Nemo* when Dory kept forgetting that she was on an adventure with Nemo. She would turn around and tell him to stop following her. Such a great movie.

I can't remember if Sadie or Sasha remembered to use the bathroom while outside, but they did manage to get utterly muddy thanks to the rain from the night before. It was more important that they have a positive experience. Stacking up positive experiences will leave little room for all their emotional baggage. Or so I thought.

After we repeated the drama with the back door, the girls hightailed it to their room and dove for the crate. They spent the rest of their first day in their crate with the door open on a very soft bed, just watching. Like classic mobsters in an old black and white movie, they preferred to have their backs against the wall so they could see who was coming and so no enemy could sneak up behind them. Sasha stayed in the back of the crate and liked to rest her head on Sadie's rump. Sadie did not relish being the front dog, but she took one for the team. I can only imagine how tense they were. I could hear what they were saying loud and clear. "Just because this bed is soft does NOT mean I trust you." Every now and then, that natural puppy curiosity would get the best of them and they would venture out. But like mermaids or fairies, if I looked at them, they would bolt back into their crate. In hindsight, it probably would have been best to foster them separately. But since they were so bonded, separating them seemed cruel. The problem with keeping them together was that they reinforced each other's negative emotions in the beginning. Positive ones, too, but those were more rare.

I spent the rest of the day on the guest bed setting up a blog for Sadie and Sasha so we could document their progress and have a marketing tool. At least, that was the plan. First, though, we had to get them ready for adoption. Rob and I had cleared our calendars for the entire weekend, which was a good thing because the dogs needed constant supervision and a constant flow of hot dogs. (Hot dogs, cut into very small pieces, are a treat it is almost impossible for real dogs to pass up. We needed to teach them that people meant food. Yummy food.) Usually on weekends we go to the gym and swim and do errands and yard work and other things that keep us tied to the treadmill of modern life. But not this weekend. And for that alone, we knew we should be grateful. In a way, it was like a vacation.

That afternoon, the girls and I tried to go outside again. This time I tossed pieces of hot dog out the door to encourage them to cross the threshold on their own. It worked, because hot dogs really are magic. By the end of the day, the dogs had learned to always nose the human's hand to check for hot dogs. (And then if moved very slowly, we could pet their incredibly soft fur with the other hand.) If you are looking to gain the trust of the dog, nothing works like a hot dog. Dog cookies do not cut it. Later in the afternoon, we diced up an entire pack of hot dogs and placed the tidbits in a Tupperware™ container. We kept Piper and Blue inside and let the girls roam the back yard. They were enticed to visit us frequently since we had the smelly, tasty hot dogs. Then we switched with much door drama and let them explore inside and our dogs have the yard. I always stayed with Sadie and Sasha and Rob took the job of reminding Piper and Blue that they had not been replaced. Inside, Sadie would walk around the house and explore. Sasha would try to follow her, but she was also afraid to let me out of her sight, as if I would do something.

By the evening, we decided to try them with Blue. After the initial snarling incident the first night, I was unsure of how Blue would react. To be honest, I was unsure of Blue in general. But he was great. He seemed to understand exactly how to behave, and why wouldn't he, I realized later? Dogs have been meeting each other for eons without my intervention. He stood quietly, wagging his tail in a low and slow motion, turning his head and averting his eyes to show he is not a threat. Sasha sniffed, and Sadie ran around the yard, checking in every few laps with a drive-by sniff. Blue stayed in his position for about a minute and then threw himself into puppy play position (front legs extended with forelegs flat on the ground, butt in the air, big smile) and sprinted across the yard to chase Sadie. Sasha followed. It was on, and it was fun.

We then added Piper, plying her with as many hot dogs as we had given the girls earlier. She wasn't happy about the new arrivals, but she was starting to associate them with getting hot dogs. (Every time Sadie or Sasha came near, I gave everyone a fistful of hot dog pieces.) So, we were in a calm-ish situation, as you can see:

From left to right: Sadie, Sasha (with a toy in her mouth) and Piper.
Checking each other out.

The rest of the weekend passed in a blur. I'm pretty sure I never actually took a shower: there just wasn't that kind of time. By Sunday night, we were sort of a family. We had spent the day outside with a lot of hot dogs – after the hailstorm, the weather gods blessed our shaky operation with blue skies and 60-degree temperatures. Blue and Sadie and Sasha would chase each other in the back yard, and Piper would watch. We quickly nicknamed Piper "She Who Does Not Play." We alternated that nickname with "the Fun Police." The dogs figured it out and ignored her *most* of the time, which was to her liking. Eventually, and to Piper's great dismay, Sasha took to sleeping on her, and Piper would look at me with eyes that said: "Exactly what did I do to deserve this?" But she tolerated it; she just wanted to make sure she got credit.

The girls were still pretty awful at coming in and out of the house. Apparently in their imaginations, the backdoor threshold was an open fire pit with dragons. Or maybe they were just worried we would attack them with a towel again like on their first night. I'm not totally sure. Either way, it was both a little funny and sad to watch them try to muster up the guts to enter and exit the house. They looked like little kids facing the steps to the high dive. Of course, if Rob was anywhere near the doorway, all bets were off. Men can be scary to dogs; they are usually bigger and have deeper voices and more upright posture.

It was amazing how in some ways they went from zero to 60 mph in just two days. Maybe not 60, but they were definitely in second gear by Sunday night. They wanted to be normal and balanced; I think all dogs do. Dogs are well and truly domesticated. Every now and then I realize that when I reach into a strange dog's kennel to take him out for a walk or a romp. Especially if it is a new and large dog. Here is a dog wrenched from what he knew (even if it was the streets, at least he knew it) stuck in a kennel and surrounded by other barking dogs and lots of smells. A perfect recipe for stress. And I don't know about you, but I often forget to be kind and appropriate and gentle when I am stressed. Yet I have never been bitten or even really afraid. Sure, there have been some dogs I don't walk, but on the whole, a strange dog with big teeth is more than happy to be led around by 125 pounds of slightly nervous me. It astounds me, and I am grateful for it.

So Monday morning I was supposed to take them back to the shelter, our job having been completed. We had proven they were not aggressive and that they could (and wanted to) function in a home.

I think Rob said it first: "There is no way we can take them back." I threw my arms around him, which of course made the dogs panic and bark. He understood! But now we were committed. To what, we didn't quite know yet. Plus since it was Monday, Rob had to go back to work. So did I, but I worked at home. He literally left. Me. At home with four dogs. Four dogs who were still finding out who each other was.

Sadie, still unsure and a little off balance.

Chapter 5 – It All Started with Little Mo

Sadie and Sasha were not the first. Oh, no. No one starts out in the major leagues. Well, maybe some do, but not me. I start at the bottom. I am not blessed with any sort of natural talent for anything. Plus, I am a slow learner. But I do, for better or worse, have a lot of guts.

A couple of years earlier, in 2009, I found myself at work at the CASPCA, afraid to go into the bathroom because there was a wild and vicious dog named Little Mo hiding behind the toilet. (So much for guts.) Actually, they said he was a dog, but he seemed more of a hybrid species to me. He had the coloring of a hound, the attitude of a fox, and the teeth of a wolverine. To get him to the shelter, animal control officers had to set a humane trap, catch him in the trap and then get him out of the trap. To get him out, they had to slide a catch-pole around his neck and drag him out. The whole thing made me think again of those scenes in *Wild Kingdom* involving helicopters and dart guns and pith helmets. Why exactly he was released into the bathroom, I'll explain in a minute.

I had a more immediate problem. You try and take your pants down and expose your plump, pink cheeks and other bits you'd like to keep intact as a growling, chigger-covered brown and white hellhound crouching inches from your behind.

But I needed to pee and had no desire to risk a kidney infection or wet my pants. I already had enough diverse and stinky bodily fluids on me that day from working with dogs.

This is Little Mo's intake photo. He may not look fierce here, but trust me. Note the black dots in his crate – chiggers and fleas.

So I stepped over the baby gate we installed at the bathroom's threshold and tried to look non-threatening as I approached the porcelain throne. I moved as slowly and as quietly as possible. I silently cursed the loud snap on my pants. And why are zippers so darn noisy? I managed to disrobe sufficiently and perched myself at the very front of the toilet. I closed my eyes both in relief and because I didn't want to see an attack coming. I finished and opened my eyes and peered behind me. The dog was still there, backed by his own choice deep into the corner. His eyes were shooting daggers at me, though, and I could see the growl start in his throat before I could hear it. I had pressed my luck enough. I reached for the toilet paper which was of course positioned slightly behind me and closer to the dog. Not a good move. He snapped at my hand and I pulled it away just in time. I then levitated off the toilet and hitched my drawers up in one motion and was over the baby gate like an Olympic hurdler, feeling momentarily saddened that my proudest athletic moment came was fueled by pure cowardice.

Great. Susanne was in the hall laughing at me.

"You just have to grab him and hold him. He'll stop growling," she said.

"Yeah, whatever. I just had to pee."

"No, seriously, come on."

Oh, goody. Another teachable moment, I thought.

So the reason this vicious, wild dog was in the bathroom held back by only a baby gate (something that can keep a toddler from falling down the stairs will keep 25 pounds of "I want to kill you" safely imprisoned? Seriously?) was that we were trying to socialize him. And by we, I mean Susanne. My boss was a nut, but I loved that about her. I never did function well in regular offices with regular people, and the shelter is where you end up when you love animals and real life is too normal. Although I did miss the bathrooms in those nice office towers. So anyway, the point of the baby gate was to allow the dog to see people coming and going and get used to us. As if proximity alone would tame the beast.

Susanne stepped over the baby gate and I followed her back into the bathroom like Shaggy would follow Scooby Doo into the haunted house. I was busy calculating the odds of repeating my gold medal hurdling effort. Before I could voice my doubts, she reached behind the toilet and grabbed Little Mo by the scruff of the neck and pulled him out. She moves quickly. He tried to bite her, but the way she had his head, he couldn't. His eyes were as big as saucers, but he seemed to have decided since biting wasn't working, he'd just freeze. Susanne kept him in this submission hold for a few minutes and then put him back. He scampered behind the toilet with a look that said "That will NEVER happen again." Susanne was un-fazed.

I noticed my fly was still open, so I zipped myself up.

"See? He'll get used to us eventually. If he wanted to really bite me, he would have."

Little Mo never did bite anyone, and a week later, this dog had shed his fear and loathing of us along with his chiggers. It would take a while before he started spending his days bounding from office to office like a politician campaigning for votes.

All fixed up!

The saddest and happiest day was when he got adopted. Without compassion, patience, and the resources to give Little Mo the time and attention he needed, the world would have been deprived of a very special little dog who ultimately made a family very happy.

It was enough to make you believe in miracles. We all considered keeping Little Mo as an office dog, but decided he deserved a family of his own. You have to learn pretty darn quickly not to be selfish in this business.

So you can see how it all started with Little Mo. If he can be saved, anyone can, I figured. He was the gateway drug and I was the sixth grader starting with huffing glue and graduating to crystal meth. After that, whenever I saw a growling, terrified dog at the shelter, I was drawn to him like a moth to a flame. I quickly developed an iron bladder and consistent hurdling skills. After Little Mo, I felt able to branch out on my own.

So I picked Walter. An exuberant Malamute / German Shepherd mix - or so we guessed, Walter was 95 pounds of "Let's go!" He looked like a wolf. I gravitated to Walter at first because I pitied him. It was August when he came to the shelter. August in the south. His fur was a foot long and dense; it seemed he had never been brushed. Everyone was intimidated by him. He didn't really do anything wrong, he was just so big and unruly. Well, if you had the misfortune of being short, he might playfully put his mouth on your head. He wouldn't close his mouth; he just wanted to see if he could fit your head in his mouth. It was like he was doing it on a dare. But if you were a scaredy-cat in addition to being short you might go wailing to the front desk about how he needed to be pulled off the adoption floor. (She didn't last long at the CASPCA.)

This put him in a bit of trouble. But I liked him and I didn't like desk work, which my job as Volunteer Coordinator required a lot of, so I tried to help. He clearly had never been petted or really known humans to be helpful. There was little chance he would get better in isolation. He needed exercise and exposure, but he wasn't sure how to communicate what he wanted. He didn't understand our language. I got through to him by brushing him. Often dogs seem aloof or unfriendly or even aggressive because they are uncomfortable. Some have never really been petted or even touched. With a curry comb (a flexible metal oval with shallow teeth often used on horses) and a hairbrush, I took three shopping bags full of hair off him one afternoon. The result was like that fairy tale my mom loves – the one where the mouse removes the thorn from the lion's paw. Walter was ecstatic and instantly trainable. He looked to me for everything because I had fixed his matted fur. So I started bringing him to the volunteer room where I worked – even though he wasn't a terribly good office dog (he liked to mark his territory in addition to the size issue). I fantasized about adopting him, but didn't think the fit would quite be right between Blue and this big, dominant dog. Nor did I think he would literally fit in our house. So, I just kept advocating for him, lurking on the adoption floor, pouncing on anybody who looked at big dogs. Months went by. I kept brushing him and trying to keep him happy and tired. (Tired dog = good dog!)

Walter at the shelter. Those eyes.

Winter came, which helped a lot - at least he wasn't so hot. But it also upped his energy level, and he liked to run. I could manage running with him uphill or on the flat sections of the trail that encircled the CASPCA, but on the downhills, I couldn't stop him. I often had to grab the fence on the downhill portion of these "walks" to stop from careening down the hill.

Walter did eventually get adopted by a family with a lot of land who loved his oddness and didn't mind his mouthiness. They knew enough about dogs not to confuse the mouthiness with biting. And they had no tiny toddlers in the home to worry about Walter accidentally fitting in his mouth. [2] But first we had the snowstorm to end all snowstorms.

It was the first week of December, and we got two feet of snow. It surprised everyone, and only a few people could get to work. I only lived three miles from the shelter so I offered to walk to work and help clean cages and medicate animals. When I was done with those exhausting chores, I decided to break some trail for the volunteers who would probably start coming in as soon as the roads were cleared to walk dogs. I came up with a brilliant plan for the work, too. I would use Walter to help. His big chest could break the trail, and I could just walk behind him. My plan had a flaw, though. Walter was definitely happy to see the snow: "Thank God! I've been hot since I was born!" he said with his eyes and tail and ears. But his happiness led to bounding instead of walking which meant all four paws would spring free of the earth and plunge into the snow five feet down the trail. I was the one who broke trail at a running clip trying to keep up with him. I thought my heart was going to explode. He kept looking back at me. "Why are you going so slow!" I miss Walter.

Then Star showed up. With one blue eye and one brown eye and her skinny brown and white body, she crawled right into my heart and parked herself there. She put on the emergency brake and everything. Star arrived at the shelter in full-blown heat in the freezing cold of late February. I wanted to foster her as well, but the staff veterinarian said bringing home a dog in heat could drive my

---

[2] Sadly, this home ended up not working out three years later. These things happen, and they break your heart.

(neutered) male crazy. Since that was to be avoided, I set out to help her *in situ.*

I spent hours in her kennel, feeding her hot dogs and canned food. I brought her special blankets and toys. The other dogs next to her were not at all happy with all the attention Star was getting. I felt terribly guilty, but you love who you love, and I had learned more about myself. I had to narrow my focus to survive shelter work. If I thought about all the dogs in the shelter, I'd go mad. Luckily, there were other people with the skills to do just that who had no inclination to sit with a terrified pit bull. After her bleeding slowed down, meaning her heat cycle was coming to an end, I started bringing her up to the volunteer room so she could learn to be around other people and get warm.

The CASPCA volunteer room was a large room with two doors. It was hard to keep them shut because it was a public room, not my private office. People had to come in and out to sign in for their volunteer shifts and to get a variety of stuff that ended up stored in the room. While Star did not seem to be a biter, she was a bolter. Had any door stayed open long enough, she would have bolted out. I kept her in a crate much of the time to reduce stress on everyone and to help her get used to people. Slowly, she got used to me and let me pet her even in open spaces. She did not, however, cotton to anyone else at first. Like Sasha would eventually do, she went from terrified of me to protective of me. But it wasn't about me personally. I was just a resource that she wanted to keep for herself, having probably never had anything worth keeping before and being terribly afraid that she would lose it. I had to get her used to other people. So I would carry her over to whoever came in and force her into their arms. It was risky, but I was pretty confident nothing bad would happen. I was right; she was all bluster.

Star was eventually adopted, but she bolted from her new owner's home and went missing for four days. They found her, and after that rough start, everything seemed fine. But whew. Couldn't anything be easy?

Star in my office. Those eyes.

Chapter 6- "Maybe This Isn't So Bad"

To my mind, Sadie and Sasha's combination of fear and desire was universal. Maybe not in what they feared or desired, but in the fact that they both feared and desired *something*. The same thing. I have felt the simultaneous pull of opposite emotions, the conflict of being afraid of what I most wanted and wanting that which frightened me terribly. And then changing my mind. Everyone has these feelings in different proportions and with different objects or outcomes. In some, the combination can be explosive; in others, it is just sad. It depends on the objects of your fear and desire. Dogs are far simpler than humans both in what they fear and what they desire, but the basics are the same. They fear loss and pain, and they desire love and freedom. Just like us. The list could obviously be expanded upon, but you get the picture.

Well, after the first few days with the girls, it was getting easier in our house, although having four dogs when you are used to two is definitely *more*. Sixteen legs versus eight. Twice as much poop is a lot of poop, and twice as much food is a lot of food. Gradually, over the first week, Sadie and Sasha learned that life isn't so bad. They also learned how to run, that the couch is the *deal*, and how to come in and out of the house without terror. Fear yes, but not terror. They discovered that they love ice cream and cereal bowls. They had not yet learned to go for a walk, though. "For God's sake, woman, we just finished deciding you are not scary. Give us a minute," they seemed to say whenever I would try to attach a leash.

"Outside? In the cul-de-sac? That is a HUGE space! Who knows what could get us there. No, that is scary out there. We are not budging." So we spent a lot of time sitting on the front step just looking.

A week in, housetraining was not quite finished, either. But so long as you didn't startle them, they let themselves be petted, and they seemed to enjoy it. Although Sasha's little body hadn't yet relaxed one bit. Her muscles stayed tight as a drum. Sadie was just a looser personality. They were both still jumpy, but more easily reassured. And they were learning some self-starting skills.

Sasha's hairy eyeball would reappear, though, whenever Rob was near a doorway for the next several weeks. It was a combination of bluster and fear; it was the expression of a bully. Sadie just would turn and run if Rob was in the doorway. No hairy eyeball, no chance to explain. Just flight. For a while, Rob felt pretty bad about himself.

Sadie wondering where we are.

As I tried to explain to him, a lot of shelter dogs are afraid of men. Men are tall and big and have deep voices. It actually took about a month for them to be completely at ease with Rob. (And then he wore a hat one day and that nearly ruined everything. You could see and hear the alerts going off in their heads. "Aaah! Who is that man in the hat?")

As we were all adjusting emotionally, and it was time to make adjustments to the house to make daily life easier. For the record, putting a sheet over the rug is a great way to locate pee spots quickly. Sadie was the problem in this area. She would forget to pee while she was outside, charmed by a butterfly or something, and then come in, realize she had to pee, and squat wherever she was.

Sasha got housebroken pretty quickly. For better *and* worse, Sasha didn't forget things.

We knew they weren't ready to be adopted yet, but we thought it wouldn't be long. I mean they were young adorable and happy in our home already. This was cake, and weren't we going to be the heroes? While I have always disliked the term "rescue dog," I was feeling pretty heroic. And smug. I had certainly habituated Sadie and Sasha to being kissed and manhandled. Note to self – smug is a precursor to nothing good.

Now, back to the positive. The power of the hot dog in this whole process simply cannot be overstated. I learned from Charlottesville dog trainer Karen Quillen about the magical power of hot dogs. (Speaking of Karen, it was she who, along with my boss Susanne, gave me the confidence to work with dogs beyond my abilities. All you need is a role model. It's like being the second person to eat a lobster.) I initially fought the hot dog lesson. Those hot dog pieces are slimy and make your hands stink. But dry dog biscuits, no matter how fancy and convenient, won't do it. At the shelter, there are always boxes of biscuits around thanks to donations. However, they are usually stale because so many people come in and out of the place and closing the box just doesn't happen. To some dogs, a stale dog biscuit is just fine, thank you very much. To others, it is simply insufficient.

By the end of that first week, we had managed to go for a "walk" or two. I put *walk* in quotation marks because it usually stopped halfway down the stairs of our front yard, or at the most by our neighbor Roger's mailbox. Still, it was progress. The girls were racing around the backyard and developing some pretty cute habits.

Sasha had taken to jumping on the little metal table next to the grill which was under the kitchen window if I wasn't outside with her. I would be washing dishes and a little white and black Sasha head would appear at my eye level. Then, of course, the whole cheap table would crash down, and Sasha would leap off. I'd go outside to see if she was scared, and she would be rewarded for her trick. "I got the human to come and play with me! Woo-hoo!" We never could get her to stop jumping on that table, even though we were constantly worried she would hurt herself.

Here is what I wrote in the blog to summarize their first five days and celebrate their achievements (and entice adopters):

Things We Are Not Afraid Of

1) Hail. Apparently it freaked out my foster parents, though.
2) Thunder. We notice it, but it's no big deal. We are a pair of tough girls.
3) Kong toys filled with peanut butter.
4) Dinner
5) Breakfast
6) Belly rubs
7) Toys

Things We Are Still Afraid Of

1) Thresholds, particularly coming into the house. Once we're across we're fine. Sasha is a little more nervous, but hot dogs help.
2) Sudden movements. But we recover. And we don't snap. Ever.

3) Wide open spaces. Except in the back yard. Love the back yard. But sometimes we like to sit with our backs against the fence so no one can sneak up on us. Like mobsters or the guys in the old Westerns.

Things We're Getting Better At

1) Walking on a leash. Although sometimes we wonder why you are following us.
2) Coming into the house and out of our crate.
3) Approaching people.
4) Running. This is new to us. we like it. Almost as much as napping.

As you can see, I emphasized the positive a little, but I was so impressed with how far they had come so quickly. They acted more like three-month old puppies than the adolescents they were. They were learning so much so fast, and all of it was good. Because they seemed so malleable, we thought the finish line was clearly visible.

That particular finish line turned out to be a mirage.

Chapter 7 – It Helps if You Marry Well

As you probably already figured out, I am a 'plunge into things' kind of person. So far, though, when I am in over my head, I have been able to kick my way back to the surface or find a pocket of air to breathe. I am also a 'quit while I am ahead and then don't look back' kind of person. I'm not so good at finishing. I had a lot of half-finished scarves in the closet until I finally gave away my knitting needles and let the cats have the yarn. Finishing is hard. Yes, at my age, that is a little embarrassing to confess.

Rob is more of a 'consider things from all angles' kind of person, but he accepts the consequences of my plunging with grace and good humor, so long as I still make a little time for him. We make a good pair. I got lucky to find a husband who puts up with my impetuous animal decisions. (He does ask me to restrict the number of life-changing ideas I have to one a year. That seems fair enough, but it is hard.) I think he also got lucky to find someone who forces his heart to be hurt more often than he would like. Any time you do something powerful together, you add more mortar to the bricks of the foundation that holds up your relationship. Loving creatures as needy as Sadie and Sasha brought us together like being parents of a special needs child. Yes, I just compared dogs to children. I know the challenges are very different in many ways, but there is an overlap. To deny that is to deny the universality of life and need and love.

Rob is a big, strong, quiet guy - not usually gushy. Sadie and Sasha made him gushy. Here he is, ostensibly teaching the dogs the "Look" command, but really bribing them to get on his lap with a piece of hot dog..

After seventeen years of marriage, it helps to see your spouse afresh. Based on our experiences, I would suggest that fostering dogs can strengthen your marriage. Of course, how he treated my three cats when we met is a big part of why I married him in the first place.

We were living together in our first house when Jackson, one of my – well, by then, our – cats had a stroke. It was horrible. We took him to the vet who explained it would probably happen again and it would probably kill him. I can't remember the details of his medical condition; I just remember the sadness of hearing the death sentence. Jackson was a big, goofy, white cat who loved to eat watermelon. He probably was a little wacky from a knock on the head he got as a kitten. Maybe that was what led to his condition, the name of which I cannot remember for the life of me. Anyway, he was my favorite cat of my three because he was the oddball. I was ready to be there for him. I told myself I would make his last months as good as possible. I would be there at the end, I vowed. But I wasn't.

When Jackson had his second and fatal stroke, I panicked. He was in screaming pain. It was truly a nightmare. I shut down. Rob scooped him up and held him as he died. He may not go out seeking problem animals to take care of, but when they appear under his nose, those animals are damn lucky. So, it helps to marry well.

Here is my list of things beyond having a helpful and understanding partner that I found make managing a multiple-dog household easier. There are certainly differing opinions on many of these, but I think they make a good starting point for consideration.

One Crate them, and do not leave them uncrated at home alone. Some people think crating is cruel. They are incorrect, assuming your crate is large enough and you provide for all your dog's needs while she is in it. And of course, do not leave your dogs in crates for too long. (What is too long? It depends on the dog, but more than 8-10 hours is probably too long for many dogs.) I say if your dog gets enough mental and physical exercise, enough belly rubs and cuddle time, and enough food and water, crate when you need to. It's like the airlines say, put your own oxygen mask on first.

It is easy to be driven nuts by four dogs, no matter how wonderful and soft and sweet-smelling they are. And when you have four dogs who don't know each other well, it is better to be safe than sorry. So get the properly sized crate, do not leave them for a long time, and make sure there is water and a comfy bed and safe toys. Of course, Sadie and Sasha always spilled their water when I let them out, but it was a small price to pay for peace of mind. I have heard enough stories of people who had a seemingly happy three dog household when they left for work and one day came home to a dead dog. Dogs can develop a pack mentality and bad behavior can come out of boredom. Piper and Blue did not need to be in crates anymore, although we did crate Blue for the first year we had him. It also helped give the cats some freedom and made life easier for me. The more you can do to make your life easier, the more dogs you can help.

Two A top-quality, huge-capacity washing machine. With four dogs and sixteen mud-loving paws, many things need to be washed. Often.

Three Hide (or don't have) precious things. Really, is the Queen about to visit? Are photographers from *House and Garden* lining up outside your home? Make your peace with mess.

Four Nature's Miracle ™ – buy it by the case. Pee and poop are part of the game. There will be enough to frustrate you. Don't add cleaning to the list.

Five Throw away all your rawhides. I was able to give Piper and Blue rawhides because they had figured out after living together for several years that they got their needs taken care of. Stupid me thought it would be okay to give all four dogs a nice rawhide treat on a sunny afternoon. The growling started immediately; I don't even know who was first. I snatched all the rawhides away and vowed to not do that again. Toys are okay, maybe. When I worked at the shelter and we would dog-test the new dogs, we would pick up all the toys in the outdoor play areas and toss them over the fence. Better safe than sorry.

Six Feed them well and at regular times, but feed them separately. For the same reason they shouldn't have tasty treats, they shouldn't be set up to fail over food. Sadie and Sasha were sure of nothing, including getting another meal. Not only were they thin, they had not been socialized with other dogs. What should you feed them? You can find a hundred answers to that question on the internet, but in general, you get what you pay for. Avoid corn. We feed our dogs Sammy Snacks™ and once the girls started eating that, their coats got shinier, their poop got smaller (and better smelling – no joke) and they ate well and quickly without leaving food. When you have to separate dogs to eat, it's best if the dogs are prompt eaters.

Seven Use harnesses instead of attaching your leash to their collar. A scared dog wants to bolt on a walk and a harness keeps them from choking themselves to death. Or slipping out of their collars.

Eight I've made the point before, but it bears repeating: hot dogs are magic. Some people will say never feed your dog human food. I say good luck training your dog without hot dogs. And it was an ice cream bowl that made Sadie and Sasha first trust us.

Nine Clear your calendar, and ask everyone else in your life to please not have a crisis that requires your attention. Thank them for their understanding, and pay it back when it is their turn. But don't feel bad about ignoring everything else in your life for a while.

It's worth it.

Sadie and Sasha accepting their first kisses from me.

Chapter 8 – Becoming Themselves

Among aficionados of the "breed," pit bulls are renowned for their smiles. When they look at you with that smile, you feel special. Maybe it goes back to reading too many children's fantasy books about communicating with magical animals. Actually, I'm sure it does. But whatever the reason, I love pit bull smiles. The trick is that a pit bull smile doesn't always look like a human smile or a Golden Retriever smile. When Sasha smiled, she looked like she was about to sneeze. Or snarl. She looked somewhat like an alligator. We called it "Sasha's ugly face". But by process of elimination we knew it was a smile since she used it even when she didn't sneeze, and she never actually bit anything. It helped that crazy tail-wagging would accompany her ugly face. She couldn't help it that she looked crazy when she smiled. It was really her most charming feature, and it started showing up with regularity about a week into our adventure with her. Score one for Sasha in the smile department.

Less charming was her habit of barking at our neighbors. It was an alert bark, based on her fear. She was saying: "I see you and you had better stay over there." The problem was, the neighbors had no desire to approach a barking dog, so Sasha felt powerful and got her way. Also, we liked our neighbors and wanted to spend time with them. This was not good. Although it was mighty scary and required some understanding neighbors, I learned to pick her up and shove her at people, like I did with Star. "Oh, okay," she seemed to say. "If you don't think they are scary, I'll hush up."

Along with her strange and singular smile, Sasha had a unique way of walking. She walked like a greenhorn cowboy who had been in the saddle a little too long. Her head kind of lowered when she walked too, so in addition to those bow legs, she had a sad sack air about her. Running normalized everything about her.

While not really noticeable until a couple of weeks in, we discovered that by nature, Sasha was a follower. She still liked to have her own say, even if it was the same as that of whoever she was following. She was like the annoying but loveable and nerdy sidekick in a kids' movie. The leader would stand up to the bully, and then Sasha's character would say "Yeah! And don't come round here no more!" Then she'd make sure she was behind the brave kid. She had such a push-pull in her nature, it made you ache for her. Who doesn't sometimes want opposites? It must have felt so confusing for her.

Sadie, on the other hand, was never confused, although oddly she often looked totally addled. It was a cute look for a pit bull, or indeed any dog. She was also a loner. Once she figured out that her needs were being consistently met and that she was having some fun, she was often content to be in a different room from me. Sasha could never be separated. She was like a suckerfish or a barnacle or a limpet. There always, like a shadow. It was wonderful to see Sadie's independence flourish, and it was also fun (and ego-flattering) to have a shadow. They were a nice mix.

Sadie's most amusing habit was her need to play with the cat bed. Amusing for me, but not the cat. Since it was just Rob and me in the house, we occupied only two of the four chairs at our dining room table. We were able to sacrifice one chair to Skye who accepted it as a poor substitute for actually getting on the table and hovering over our dinner plates. The problem was that her cat bed is made of fleece, as are many dog toys. We have a toy box filled with dog toys, but Sadie was an explorer. Why take the easy route? She was very pleased when she first pulled the cat bed off the dining room chair. I was not, however, and told her to let go and replaced the bed with an acceptable toy and a pat on the head. Sadie would spit out the toy and retrieve the cat bed as soon as I sat down. We went through a few more rounds of this until she gave up. But the next day, she would try again – whether or not Skye was in her bed. It displeased Skye greatly to be woken from her nap by an earthquake. It also displeased Sadie to have to endure such caterwauling. We learned to intervene before Sadie got near the chair.

Next to playing with the cat bed, Sadie most enjoyed moving shoes. Not chewing them, just moving them and sometimes hiding them. After those two games came our least favorite, called "I Just Need to Bite Your Head a Little." We'd be sitting on the couch together and Sadie would suddenly want to see if she could fit your head into her mouth. She wasn't actually biting, just putting her mouth on your skull, like Walter did. Still, it was not fun for us since her teeth did come into contact with our heads. But she was determined, like with the cat bed.

As for her walk, it was also odd. Since these girls had not gotten any exercise their first months of life, it made sense their parts might have grown in a little odd. The best way to describe Sadie's walk is that she walked like she was borrowing her mother's high heels in an effort to look fancy for the boys. "Parading around," I believe it is called when a mother yells at her 13 year old. She ran, on the other hand, like a tweedy English professor chasing his hat. Which, come to think of it, looks vaguely similar.

So the biggest challenge of having four dogs in April is that four dogs make sixteen paws to wipe mud off of. "April showers bring May flowers." Bah! I would have been so happy for a couple of days without rain. The first weekend after the hailstorm was great, but then it rained at least every other day. I wanted to Astroturf the backyard, but Rob nixed the idea for aesthetic and bank account reasons. Sadie and Sasha still thought the towel was trying to kill them, so they were not first in line to have their feet cleaned. Not that I was worried about maintaining a showplace; no my house was dirty, and I regularly went into the world ungroomed. Sometimes even unwashed, particularly when my spare time was consumed with meeting the diverse needs of four dogs, two of whom were not even mine. But, it was nice to keep the big clods of mud outside.

At least now, over a week into this adventure the girls were having fun. Maybe not all the time, but some of the time. I tried to work with the camera at the ready. I was ferociously updating the blog and Facebook to get the girls' story out and make people interested in adopting them. At first, I couldn't do this because we didn't know they would make it. Now, I was getting into the swing of it like a used car salesman on late-night TV. I wanted to keep the girls in sight, both to monitor peeing and to make sure any squabbles didn't develop. Sasha seemed to have made it her mission to win Piper over. So I had to be alert for any signs of Sasha-fatigue from Piper. Not that Piper ever did anything other than voice her displeasure, but still. I was nervous. And I wanted to keep my nerves from the dogs because they can pick up on these things. It was all exhausting, and a good challenge.

But I'd be lying if I didn't admit that the biggest hurdle to getting any work done is that all I wanted to do was play with them. Sadie and Sasha were getting better each minute, learning new things and interacting on a more intimate level. Even though they still had a lot of fear – or because of that - they wormed their way into our hearts. Their curiosity was probably the most charming thing about them. Rob was in love, and I loved seeing him reduced to Jello by these nutty girls. No one has ever been or will ever be as happy to see us as those dogs are at 5am each morning. Their tails wagged so hard that their heads make little figure eights of joy.

So the first week or so of being outnumbered four to one was mostly manageable, and then Rob came home with the news he was going to have to go out of town on business the next week. Luckily, after seeing my face, the next day he talked his way out of it.

"I can't stay overnight," he told his boss, "I can't leave my wife alone with four pit bulls." People seemed to understand, and the crisis was averted. Rob understood that I needed to be able to hand off some dog supervision in the evenings, and I don't think he really wanted to miss anything. We were settling in.

Sasha making the watering can into a toy. It had a hole in it anyway.

PART TWO: Enjoying the Ride, Bumps and All

Chapter 9- Where Am I and How Did I Get Here?

One day, a couple of weeks into our adventure with Sadie and Sasha, I started thinking about the path we took to get here and the dogs who travelled it with us. I realized, lying on the bed in a pile of four dogs, that each experience led us to exactly this point. No other choice was possible after living the life we had. At least it seemed that way. So let's take a trip in the way-back time machine, to a time before wrinkles and mortgages and smart phones, and I'll show you.

Like many ignorant, dewy-eyed young couples, Rob and I got a puppy when we moved in together to cement and celebrate our wondrous love. We were living in Atlanta at the time; it was 1994. This puppy, a Boxer so god-like in his perfection we named him Thor, even carried the rings in our wedding a year later. Cute, right? Really, Thor was the perfect dog. He house-trained himself, never barked unless he absolutely had to, and was friendly and patient with strangers. He let the neighbor's Sheltie herd all 80 pounds of him by the lip because, you know, she really needed to. Thor just went along to get along. He was a better citizen of the world than either Rob or I ever could be. We were really more fans than owners.

We were allowed to purchase our brand new puppy in 1992 for $500 only after we had been fully vetted. No Supreme Court justice or presidential cabinet member ever went through such rigorous screening. We were clearly not the first ones to love Thor.

We had to explain what would happen to the dog if we split up. We only were allowed to purchase him in the end because he was flawed. Otherwise, he would have been sold to an owner who would take him to compete him in dog shows. But, Thor was unshowable since he was cryptorchid. (His testicles hadn't "descended." They were there, they were just shy.) Yet, just in case, we had to sign a contract saying we would massage his testicles to see if they would descend, and if they did before he was a year old, we would have to allow the breeders to show him. (He was *that* beautiful.) We signed, but did not massage. He was not going to leave our sight. Those testicles were staying up there if we had to use duct tape. After he turned one year old, we had him neutered. End of drama. Both of us had grown up with dogs, but Thor was OUR first dog and we obsessed. It was a joy to grow up with him.

Then into our idyll came another Boxer. The next year, a week before we were getting married, we took Thor to the vet for a check-up. He was fine and dandy, but our vet, who we adored and who was not stupid, crooked his finger and said, "Follow me."

(And why did we adore Dr. Winokur? Number one, he thought Thor was a splendid dog. Number two, and more importantly at least in the long run, he taught me how to be a responsible dog owner. You see, I have a bit of a genetic tendency to overreact. I was walking Thor around Piedmont Park when he was about three months old, enjoying the nice day and admiring stares. For the dog, not me. Then without warning, my sweet boy stopped, heaved a bit, and threw up. Ack! I hustled him home and called the vet and they saw me that afternoon. Dr. Winokur gave him a thorough examination, and asked about his stool and urine and his appetite. Finding nothing wrong, he said: "Puppies throw up. No need to panic." It was very helpful advice, but I can't say I always followed it. And he also spared the life of any spider he found in his office.)

I followed the splendid and manipulative Dr. Winokur as he took me downstairs to the surgery kennels. There, just three feet from the bottom step in the first row of kennels was a beautiful young Boxer with one eye hanging out of its socket, a leg that was reduced to hamburger meat, stiches everywhere and a piece of the trim from the car that had hit him sticking out of his neck. His owner, who had brought him into the vet's office, said he didn't want him anymore because he wasn't going to look right. This mutilated dog looked up at us and wagged his tail, and that was all she wrote. I went home and told Rob we were getting another dog. He stared at me, and I backed up and explained the situation. He agreed wholeheartedly. We made plans to take him when we got back from our honeymoon, provided he got along with Thor. Apparently this dog's name was "Rebel", but that wouldn't do. Neither Rob nor I are terribly Southern by nature, nor did Rebel need to bring much of his past with him. We renamed him Odin after the Norse god who gave up his eye for a drink from the fountain of wisdom. We always joked that Odin got shorted on the drinking part, but he was a wonderful, loving and beautiful dog.

When we brought Odin home, he took one long slow look around the place. You could see his brain do the calculations: "My house, my yard, my brother? Wowie!" He ran in circles like a tornado for a few seconds and then plopped down in the sun next to

Thor who had been watching the newcomer with a slightly stunned look on his regal face. "Who let the interloper into the kingdom?" the face seemed to say before it softened into: "Okay, as it seems to be your wish. I shall help the young one learn the ropes."

Odin was out first "used dog," and he woke up every day and said, "Thank you." Every day. He was also a little protective of me, which I quite like in a dog, I have to admit. Every time Rob raised his voice for any reason, whether at the Red Sox game or the news or me if we were having an argument, Odin would growl at him. It was funny to me, and though Rob loved Odin with all his heart, he was less amused at his silencing tactics. As Odin got older, he stopped worrying so much about raised voices.

So we went from an almost perfect puppy to a free damaged dog. Odin was still a beautiful Boxer, though. Then we moved from Atlanta to the country in Virginia. We wanted a break from city life, and we wanted a garden and as much land as we could handle. Not too long after our move, Thor was diagnosed with cancer. I will never forget the horrible sensation of falling when I got the news. It was like disengaging from reality. I had taken Thor to our new vet, who also ended up being very wonderful, because Thor seemed to be peeing a little more than usual. I expected it to be a "Puppies throw up" kind of visit like my first one with Dr. Winokur in Atlanta. Our new vet was supposed to charge me $60 and tell me that it was hot in the summer in Virginia and dogs drink more water and urinate more. End of visit. But no. Someone forgot to deliver the script. Instead, he said: "I feel something in his belly." I hated him for saying that, and my world went kind of dark at the edges. That *something* was an inoperable tumor. Thor died eight months later after a truly valiant struggle. It remains a time so sad I can hardly write about it. I still miss him desperately even though he died twelve years ago. Watching him handle each blow his cancer threw was inspiring and humbling. He would stumble, literally, then pick himself up and dust himself off. "So, this is how it's going to be," you could see him thinking. "Okay, well, I think I can handle this." And he would keep going until he couldn't.

About a year after Thor died, I was driving home one day and saw a dog in the highway. Alive. She was running in circles in the middle of the right hand lane, kind of looking like she was having fun and kind of looking completely panicked. I do not stop for dogs I see on the road. Never have, never did again. I'm too practical, at least when I am driving. But I stopped for this stinky, dirty, so-black-she-looked-green mini-pit bull–ish thing who ran from me back into the highway. Now I am scrabbling all over the interstate trying to catch this dog. I must have looked like some rube on *Hee Haw* losing a greased pig contest. Another car stops to help block traffic and keep me from getting killed.

Somehow I catch the little thing and heave her into my car. Off I go with a very happy dog. She was not shy *at all* once I had her. So I drive up the long gravel driveway, and Rob was in the front yard. I'm not sure how it all happened next, but he ends up washing her in the driveway. Odin seemed to like her, so we went for a walk. The first nasty thing she sees in the woods, she stops and rolls in. Having Boxers, who can be rather fastidious (at least ours were), this was new behavior for us. But she was just so happy, you couldn't be upset. "Got to get that bath smell off of me," she seemed to be saying.

We did the right thing and took her to the shelter in case her family was looking for her. We said we'd adopt her if no one came to claim her. But someone did. We still miss that girl.

A few years later, we moved into Charlottesville with Odin. As it turns out, we weren't country people. Well, we might have been if we'd gone "all in" and gotten a tractor. Odin loved our new house with its big, low windows facing the cul-de-sac where just enough interesting things happened to keep him from spending the last months of his life totally asleep. Odin was getting older and slowing down, so in addition to the stimulation from the neighborhood activities, I convinced myself he needed a companion to perk himself up and Rob agreed. He said he didn't want to come to the shelter and look at dogs with me. I think he was worried he couldn't handle it. "Whatever you bring home, I know I'll love."

I knew we were going to get a shelter dog because, well, I don't remember why. It just felt natural, and the shelter was close by. Well, after a home visit and $100, I brought Piper home and she changed everything. (The home visit was funny – the shelter employee took one look at the fenced yard, another at Odin on his fluffy bed by the window and checked the box on her form and left.) I met Karen, the dog trainer who taught me about hot dogs and everything else, through Piper. Karen then became my reference at the shelter. So it really was thanks to Piper I got into this wonderful mess. So let me explain a little about that sweet, nutty girl.

First, see how gorgeous she is? And that is not just my opinion. One day, Piper and I ran (literally) into football announcer Howie Long and his wife in a Charlottesville parking garage. The stairs have a huge blind spot. Anyway, his exact words were: "What a beautiful dog." And his wife quickly agreed. So there. (Ever since, I agree with everything Howie says on TV. I am loyal that way.)

However, her gorgeousness hid a troubled soul. Piper is probably a mix of pit bull and some sort of herding dog or "northern breed" (like a husky) with a dose of hound, according to our patient vet. He taught me that shelter mutts are rarely the product of two purebred dogs; they are more likely the offspring of two mutts. Having never had such a dog, and loving her with all my heart, I had to figure out how to live with her. The beginning was rocky. She barked at Rob for the first five days. Her bark can peel paint. But I was raised a good liberal. I didn't believe in the curse of genes. We can all better ourselves, even little pit bull mutts, I thought. I just needed to learn the tools to help her.

She required multiple obedience classes and private sessions with Karen, marking the beginning of my lessons on dogs. Piper does not have a lot of issues - and they are mitigated by her sheer wonderfulness - but those issues are carved deeply into her being. There was no quick fix. "You know, she's a happy dog," Karen said to reassure me once we realized Piper didn't play and would rather most dogs keep their distance. Karen also said "It's a good thing you got her." Karen is also trained as a human psychologist, so I am not sure if she meant it was good for me or for Piper.

You have to be on guard with Piper to protect her and the squirrels from her less noble tendencies. And not just squirrels. She doesn't like anything small that moves quickly and erratically, like children. That makes you a rather unpopular neighbor, and it removes all possibility of walking with coffee in the morning. Or while daydreaming. Constant vigilance is barely enough. She is not a good girl. Not that it is her fault, but she is afraid of thunder, hot air balloons, brush grinders, and the moon. And big dogs. But home? Home is her safe place, as it should be. We did something right. Even if she hears the tree grinders or sees the moon, she is fine in her backyard.

Odin loved Piper, and Piper loved Odin, but no other dogs. Odin only lived about six more months, but Piper seemed to take his loss in stride and seemed quite happy. Still, the thought she needed a companion took my brain hostage about a year later. I had been an employee of the shelter for two whole weeks in 2009 when we brought Blue home.

I would eventually see the phenomenon repeated many times with other new employees at the shelter. Within a week or two or at most a month, they adopt a "problem dog". (Of course Blue's only problem was that he was ugly and a pit bull mix, neither of which were real problems, but still. He fits my theory; he has to. It's my book.) I came to see it as a vaccination, a way of immunizing yourself against the emotional onslaught of all the dogs needing help. You feel powerless to help them all, so you quickly adopt one dog to regain some power. None of this is conscious. You actually think you've met your soul mate, or you're "helping" your other dog at home. Or you are getting your spouse a dog. Isadora Duncan writes that artists see the world either close up or from far away. I would say the division applies to non-artist as well. Adopting a dog quickly suited those of us who saw the world "close up."

I met Blue in my first dog meeting in the basement of the CASPCA. This was where we discussed "problem" dogs as well as all the dominant breeds, including pit bulls. We also did the rest of the temperament testing in this meeting - the dog-to-dog introductions which allowed us to see how a dog got along with other dogs. We would try and match males with females because even neutered, males and females just got along better than two females or two males. It was a rule of thumb, and there were many exceptions, but it was a good place to start. And we would try to introduce the new dog to a dog we knew pretty well.

These dog-to-dog introductions would begin with the dog at issue (he would be "at issue" because he was a new dominant breed or because he made the list of problem dogs) hanging out at the meeting. Then someone – often me – would go get the chosen playmate. We would do these introductions in a play park outside or in the basement. There'd be about six of us and we'd stand in a circle. The dogs would be on leash at first, and then if all was going well, we'd drop the leash of one dog and then the other. To the uninitiated, it could have looked like a dog fighting circle. Interestingly, I never saw any pair we introduced get into an actual fight. Sure, sometimes there would be annoying or inappropriate behavior from one dog to the other – like air snapping or barking or humping - but it rarely escalated.

At Blue's "meet and greet," (our rhyming phrase for these dog-to-dog introductions) he just flopped onto his back and showed his belly to the world. "I'm friendly and unintimidating!" he shouted with his behavior. Blue even tolerated being mounted by the bully of a female we had brought down for the test. "Perfect," I thought. "Piper can still be the boss and as crazy as she needs to be. This dog can handle her."

Blue was one of the uglier dogs at the shelter with his dull brindle coat, an underbite you could jam a fist into, as well as bat

Blue in our yard, begging me to throw the ball instead of taking a stupid picture.

ears and a lazy eye. But he so clearly just wanted to be loved. His personality was dazzling. Piper, on the other hand couldn't care less if anyone other than Rob and I loved her. (And for her first couple of years, she wasn't that worried about Rob.) But Blue was campaigning for love, so for some reason, I thought that was a perfect match.

But most of all, he was just so darn happy. After years of explaining to people who wanted to pet Piper that she just wasn't much of a fan of meeting people, I wanted a friendly dog. In the stew that was our family, we needed a new ingredient. But no dog – no living creature – is defined by a single adjective. I wasn't just getting a happy dog. I was getting Blue, and Blue wasn't one-dimensional. But still, he was essentially happy, in the same way Sadie and Sasha were essentially terrified and Piper was essentially aloof.

Since Piper was not by nature a happy-go-lucky dog, I thought she could use a little of that in her life. Come to think of it, no one in our house was. Much like married couples who do best with complementary traits instead of matching ones, I decided Piper needed a dog who was strong where she was weak. And weak where she was strong. Well, I ended up with half that. Dogs change once they are in your home, once they figure out the rules. But I am getting ahead of myself, again.

I talked Rob into just "meeting" Blue, and we had a done deal. He has enough of a Boxer look that he wormed his way right into Rob's heart, reminding him – and me – of Thor and Odin, our first dogs. And I think my husband needed a boy dog. Nineteen dollars later, which was the employee adoption fee, Blue hopped in the car. I think he threw up on the way home. He has since done that several more times on car rides. Once he was home, Piper amazingly loved playing with him for a while and then looked at us as if to say: "Okay, he can go home now, I'm done."

It took months of good food and a couple of baths for his coat to acquire any noticeable sheen, and now I think Blue is the most a beautiful, round-headed, "ugly" dog. He is the best napping companion in the world, but he's not too good at sleeping in the bed. He has to sleep on your pillow. As we got to know him, he proved to be essentially that same happy dog, but there was a serious side to him. He hated to lose. At anything. He is the Michael Jordan of dogs. He is too sensitive, which mean he picks up on all your nonverbal cues, but sometimes he won't listen to your verbal ones. He is also his own dog. But he is essentially an optimist while Piper is a pessimist, so he was the perfect addition to the family. I bounce around between the two states like a mentally ill ping-pong ball.

Blue took a while to settle in. It makes me think he must have had a hard time trusting people. He was happy all the time, but he wasn't *home.* He was always ready to pack up his non-existent stuff and leave, if necessary. Maybe he never knew what a home was. Outwardly, he seemed at home, but he wouldn't make eye contact, and he wouldn't trust me and Rob completely until we went to the beach about six months later. Something just changed in him. He even stopped chasing the cats. He became gentler, too. Our cat Skye eventually trained Blue to clean her ears for her. It took a while, but she kept head-butting him in the mouth until he figured it out.

Rob and I decided we just had to share him. He really was the strongest reason "we" decided to foster, plus I was just getting used to a higher level of mess. Blue ended up being "Professor Blue". Dogs learn more from other dogs than they do from people. All dogs speak the same language after all. Blue taught Sadie and Sasha the ways of the house. Blue is a dog who approaches everything like it is a job, even play. So his job was to help them understand. Eventually, though, his good nature was severely tested by Sasha.

Chapter 10 – "You Can't Save Dogs without Loving People"

Like most people, when I love something, I want to protect it. This whole business of "when you love something, set it free" is easier said than done. And I think it's a load of hooey. If you love something, I don't know, maybe a dog, I say feed it good food and take it to the vet, and walk it and buy it a fluffy bed and play with it and put it in Fort Knox and keep it safe. That love, that protective instinct, misguided as it may be, would sometimes turn to distrust of potential adopters at the CASPCA. Okay, so maybe it was love mixed with arrogance. A kind of love that says: "I know better than you do." Love plus arrogance is always a bad combination, unless you are aiming to be King Lear. Love makes you tribal and stupid and fearful like Shakespeare's old King; it can create an "us and them" mentality. I don't know why, but I would often see tribal lines between staff and volunteers too. As Chrissy Hynde sang, "It's a thin line between love and hate."

Susanne (my boss at the CASPCA) would caution her employees not to judge potential adopters or their way of loving dogs. "You can't save dogs without loving people," she would say. She was right of course, but it was hard. Love stirs up other emotions and powerful opinions. It is messy. I often saw the worst of people, too, and it was hard not to hate them. What people will or will not do to their dogs is painful to see firsthand. It is shocking how quickly a beloved family member can become something that needs to be disposed of. We had to help people who surrendered their dogs to us because they chewed the furniture. We tried to offer solutions, but they didn't want solutions. They wanted to get rid of their dogs. We spoke of crates, of training (at a reduced cost), of all the options. "Nah, it's cruel to keep a dog in a crate," the dad would answer. "What, do you think they live here in a concrete kennel?" I wanted to scream when I heard these conversations at the front desk. But we had to be polite. Customer-focused, it was called. Even when the customer was a douche bag. It was hard.

Years ago I worked with a guy named David who thought owning a dog was a crime against humanity. Not literally, but nearly. Dog owners don't care enough about people, he argued. All that love and time and money lavished on dogs should instead go to a worthy cause, preferably one of his choosing. I hated him because I thought I had to. If it was going to be dog people versus non dog people, I had to stand up for my kind. I think about David now because I've learned how dangerous and stealthy hate is, how it can become a habit that shrinks your world to a tiny pinpoint of space with no room for anyone or anything.

Dogs came to the shelter in a variety of ways. Some were picked up by animal control. Some were strays who were wandering the streets with varying degrees of success, some were hit by cars and brought in by the people who hit them, some were surrendered as I described above, some were surrendered by the families of people who died or by soldiers being deployed to foreign wars. It was never a good time in the lives of the dogs or their owners. But 99% of the dogs were good dogs, and for some, sadly, the shelter was the best place they had been in a long time.

Take Midnight: he was a beautiful. A big, strong, black pitbull-ish dog with white markings and the softest fur. He was brought in by a woman who stole him from her neighbor because the dog was being left chained outside with a broken leg and no water in the heat of the summer. Midnight thought the shelter was awesome by the way. He got food and water and vet treatment and walks and cuddles. "Wowie!" You could just see it in his eyes. (And in case you wonder how animals get their names, we name them on intake. Sometimes the folks working the front desk will get on a roll and you'll end up with a week's worth of dogs named after Olympians or 1970s rock stars. It's funny to walk around the shelter and see the thematic threads.) Midnight ended up in a home with another dog and a woman who had a bum leg herself. It was a match made in heaven.

Then there were the people who wanted to adopt a dog you cared for but you just weren't sure it was a good idea. Maybe they fit a bad stereotype you had; maybe they didn't seem to care about anything but how the dog looked. Maybe they had too many kids. Maybe it just smelled wrong. But what if I was wrong? If the dog was going to be safe and cared for, we had to let it go. Otherwise, there is no space and dogs get euthanized. Life is better than death. It's that simple. It helps to make a good match, of course, but no one gives you a crystal ball just because you work in a shelter. And most people aren't bad. Like dogs, they just aren't perfect, but who is? You try to give them good information and hope the dog teaches them the rest.

Sometimes, people surprised you in a good way. I don't remember his name or the dog's name, but an older, fit gentleman came in looking for a dog. He had hounds in the past and was looking for another. I happened to be in the lobby when he came in, so I walked around the kennels with him and showed him the hounds. We had dozens of them. I didn't know many of them well, but there was one shy, kind of pudgy mid-sized mixed breed that we all loved. Okay, he was not just shy, he was really scared. But shy hounds are fine according to the powers that be – not like shy pit bulls. They don't tend to be potentially hiding aggression. (Not that pit bulls are, that's just the rap they get.) Hounds were just left to roam, usually hunting dogs released after the season.

This dog was not going to be an easy dog, and he was not particularly beautiful. That made two strikes against him. Somehow, though, this man and this dog clicked. Yes, this dog was going to be a giant pain in the neck. Easily spooked and probably not too housebroken (can you be too housebroken?), I can't see how anyone would pick him over all the other dogs. But sure enough, this man did. And four months later he sent me a Christmas card with a photo of him and that lucky hound sitting on the couch. The dog still looked a little suspicious, but he was snuggled right up against his new owner. The letter listed all the things the dog was terrified of: skateboards, birds, bicycles, other dogs, everything. But the man was happy. And I learned a lesson that day that I have to keep re-learning: don't let your assumptions get in the way of what you see.

Johnny was a big, young, athletic brown and white pit bull who was going a little nuts in his small kennel. In the nick of time, a young man came into the shelter specifically looking for a large brown and white pit bull. No, he hadn't lost his dog - the police had shot and killed his dog who looked a lot like Johnny. Now, every story has two or three sides, I know that, but according to this guy, there was no provocation. The officer came into his yard and shot the dog because it was loose. In the dog's own goddamn yard. I don't know what the best is way to get over something like that. You probably just have to follow your instincts and make your own way without hurting yourself or others. This young man wanted to channel his grief into helping another dog. Johnny apparently looked a lot like his old dog. Say what you want about how maybe it wasn't a good idea. Maybe this guy had too much baggage: his dog was killed only a couple of weeks ago. Still, like I said, Johnny was going nuts in his kennel. Some dogs just need more than a couple of walks a day. He was on the path to going "kennel crazy," which means he was one step away from a bad incident which would mean a trip to death row. We all wanted to get him out, at least give him a chance. He just had a lot of energy and smarts. And to go with an owner who understood pit bulls and really knew more than most of us what bad things can happen? I believed this man would keep Johnny safe give him a good life. But with pit bulls and other dominant breeds, we don't just operate on belief. We check. Johnny's new owner got a home visit a couple of days later and everything checked out. (We mostly look for evidence of dog fighting and chains.)

I got an email from Johnny's adopter a couple of months later with a photo of him and Johnny stretched out together on an old plaid couch. It made my month.

Now, don't tell, but many of the really "bad" dogs go home with employees. (Speaking of loving people, my CASPCA co-workers were amazing people. We came from all walks of life and we never really knew anything about each other than we all love animals. When you think about it, what more do you need to know?) There are three kinds of dogs that generally need the most help in the shelter: hounds, because there are a lot of them and they can be essentially feral; pit bulls, because, well, see this whole book; and LSDs, also known as "little s%#t dogs." Toy breeds usually don't end up at the shelter unless they are really, really rotten. They don't usually get loose and roam the neighborhood making trouble and babies. Nope, they are usually surrendered for biting people, or they are rescued from a neglectful or abusive situation. It is often not their fault they are LSDs. If they were large, threatening breeds, their behavior would not be tolerated. But since the damage they can inflict is minimal, we try and find them home, preferably without children and with people who get the rules these dogs come with.

Beth, a longtime employee of the CASPCA, was the champion for the LSDs. Often there would be one in her office, sharing the space with the displeased Violet, a white cat who tolerated the little dogs, barely. The office dog was usually one who could not be handled, except by Beth, and he would snarl at you with death rays shooting out of his eyes. The dog would usually be a five or six pound thing, so it wasn't too scary. They would come and go, thanks to Beth who was so easygoing herself that she undoubtedly had a calming influence on these dogs. I remember discussing problem dogs in the managers' weekly dog meeting and if they were small, the question would be: "Have you tried Beth's office?"

Heather ended up with the dog who spins in circles, but only clockwise. Susanne had up to seven dogs, including one who looks like a platypus crossed with a basset hound with a Mastiff, as well as a couple of feral dogs who won't come in her house. Puppies rotated in and out of her house on a regular basis to grow up a little and be socialized by her pack. Ashley had a formerly super shy pit bull. Many three-legged and one eyed cats go home with staff and volunteers, and Emily, the staff vet, has the worst of the scratch-and-dent cases, the chronically sick, the brain damaged, and the three-legged.

So people were both awful and wonderful. You'd see the Animal Care folks – the kennel cleaners who come and go, because they get minimum wage and it's a tough job – paying special attention to their favorites. Their favorites were usually the freaks and geeks, too. It's a secret society; all dogs force you to be your best and forgive you when you're not. But troubled dogs? They'll have a beer with you and say, "Oh, man, I've been there too." They seem to know they don't fit in. They know they are broken, just like you. They also want to believe it will be all okay. And it will, if you have a big enough heart to allow yourself pain, which makes me think of the lyrics to "That's What Makes you Strong" by Jesse Winchester

> If you love somebody
> Then that means you need somebody
> And if you need somebody
> That's what makes you weak
> But if you know you're weak

And you know you need someone
O it's a funny thing
That's what makes you strong

That's what makes you strong
That's what gives you power
That's what lets the meek come sit beside the king
That's what lets us smile
In our final hour
That's what moves our souls
And that's what makes us sing.

Chapter 11 – The Basement, the Blog and the Cats

Speaking of music, for some reason a few months before bringing Sadie and Sasha home, I decided I needed to learn to play guitar. I like to learn new things, and I wanted a hobby that didn't leave evidence of how bad I was behind, like knitting did. I never could get the hang of that: plus, it hurt my elbows. I would have perished on the prairie, or at least had a cold neck.

I enjoyed the guitar and, after a lot of practice, was making some sounds with it that were almost pleasant. The first two weeks with the girls, however, I had neither time nor energy to practice my scales. But as April was giving way to May and things were going well (meaning there were times when *all four dogs would actually be napping at the same time* and there was nothing to clean up), I decided to pick it back up. Bad idea. You try picking up a giant piece of wood and see how your scared dogs react. With one look to each other, my little foster dogs said:

"That looks like a Sadie and Sasha beating stick! Run!"

It wasn't so bad that they cowered and ran into "their" room (the guest room), it was the accusing looks they threw back at me.

"Seriously?" I wanted to say. "Have I ever hit you? Have I not proved myself yet?"

Their answer is "no, and also no." It takes a long time and some dogs never fully trust, at least not when you pick up something large that could be wielded as a weapon. Or maybe they were just not in the mood for music. I decided to wait to pursue my future as a troubadour.

As they are inclined to do, the days stretched into weeks. We had no potential adopters in sight yet, but the more immediate issue was that we had a nickname problem. As a childless couple, Rob and I have always called each other "Mom" and "Dad" to our dogs, as in: "Look! Daddy's home!" Embarrassing, maybe, but true. We knew we weren't Mom and Dad to Sadie and Sasha though. Not because they were not our *children* but because they were not our *dogs*. They were our foster dogs, and we knew we needed boundaries. The girls couldn't live with us - Piper was making that clear with her increasing lethargy - so we wanted to be careful to keep the distinctions clear. So we decided to be "Lady" and "Dude." In a way, these were the names they gave us. Sadie would say: "Lady, Lady, lady, lady," whenever she saw me in a New York cabbie's accent for some reason. Sasha would say: "Mine, mine, mine, mine," but then, that's a weird name. Both would say "Dude!" when Rob surprised them. (Yes, like Keanu Reeves in a surfer flick.) Or, so we joked to each other. Making up dialog for the dogs was a very time-consuming and delightful hobby.

Blue's schedule was full as well. As the only extrovert in the house, he was still doing the heavy lifting of teaching these dogs. He taught them how to play and how to run early on. They were very good students. For dogs who spent the first nine months of their lives in a backyard cage, they learned how to run pretty quickly, too. Now, he was working on showing them that walking around the block was not scary and that snuggling on the couch and sleeping through the night were very, very cool. In fact, despite the guitar debacle, the girls were learning so much it had to hurt, like a physical growth spurt.

We learned things, too. For example, Piper growled the whole time, but since the dogs didn't take her seriously, we realized we didn't have to either. We were learning to speak her language, and we learned from Sadie and Sasha. It was like being in a *Dr. Doolittle* movie. We also started just leaving the back door open - flies and mosquitos be damned - which finally helped the girls get over their threshold issues. Sadie and Sasha developed confidence from exploring the inside and outside as much was they wanted and when they wanted. Luckily, Sadie was about 99-percent housebroken. They did love being outside and always looked most relaxed there.

So we had the back door threshold issues covered, but the girls didn't think their new confidence should extend to any other doors. "All doors are individuals," you could hear them thinking.

(The fact they chose to mock Animal Farm Foundation's message that "All dogs are individuals," I found both deeply troubling and humorous at the same time.) So the front door was still an issue as was the door to the basement. The basement was apparently even more scary than the cul-de-sac. But it was also a perfect dog play space: vast, carpeted with cheap carpet, and nearly empty save for a few pieces of furniture we cared nothing about. We tried to entice the girls down the stairs for weeks. Sasha, who was more scared but also needed to be with you more, would stand with her head in the doorway and extend a paw, but that was as far as it got. Sadie would stick her head around the door frame, but would go no further and didn't even seem to want to.

After weeks of us begging and demonstrating how much fun Piper and Blue had down there with us (and how many hot dogs they got) one day Sasha finally took the first step! We applauded and offered loads of encouragement. But that was all we were going to get. She backed up and out. She had gone as far as she could. So we just ignored her and had noisy fun in the basement. Her curious white face returned. Two steps. Then three. Finally all the way down! She worked so hard and was so proud of herself. Hearing the attention she was getting or simply noticing her sister was missing. Sadie pranced down the steps next as if it were nothing. Another milestone, and a useful one at that. The basement was excellent for rainy day fun.

About a year earlier, I had purchased a nylon indoor camping and play set designed for kids because: a) it was cheaper than stuff for dogs, and b) I was hoping to get our dogs some indoor play options that were more mentally challenging than running around chasing each other. It had a tent, a six foot long tunnel and a hoop. But would Piper or Blue go in the tunnel? God, no. We had tried cookies, then human treats to get Blue to go through it. Piper had no interest, but then we never really expected her to. But Blue, I was sure Blue was an agility dog at heart. I thought: "What about if I put one of those little mini-snickers you buy in bags at Halloween in the middle of the tunnel, which is only like four feet long?" Nope. Not even then. Both dogs would go into the tent, but clearly wanted to file a grievance with the board. Or a protest with the judge. We were not supposed to be doing this to them. Since it wasn't fun, we put the toys away and gave up. Fine, I thought, there goes 20 bucks down the drain.

For some reason I still had the tunnel set up, and, when Sadie finally came down, she seemed to say:

"Ooooh, tunnel. Cool! I have been waiting for one of these!"

And she zipped right through it like she was born for tunnels. When she saw how pleased we were, she zipped right through it again. Now you might think Piper and Blue would have seen how easy it was – and how much it pleased us – and hustled right in next. You would be wrong if you thought this. Blue tried, but only with his front feet. His rear feet never left the carpet, the safe zone. Oh well.

We had a similar issue with walks. For Sadie and Sasha, their first journeys into the wider world began with simply making it down a few of the front steps and hanging out. But as you can see from the photo above, our house had a lot of steps.

Eventually, we got across the cul-de-sac, only to stop and huddle under our neighbor Claudia's forsythia bush. We spent a lot of time there. Luckily, Claudia liked dogs and liked us. That bush was about 60 feet from our front door and as far as I could get most days before they realized – "Crap! We're out in the open! Duck and cover!" Actually Sadie was the worst. It was the opposite of the tunnel. Sasha was better, and we tried to take her separately. Some days it worked; some days it didn't.

But you can't tell potential adopters the whole truth about their issues with walking. People want dogs they can walk. I never lied exactly, but I certainly kept the difficulties out of the blog. Here is one entry:

> I took Sasha and Sadie for a walk around the block. That may not sound like a big deal, but for these girls, who were terrified of open spaces and had clearly not spent much, if any, time walking on a leash before coming to the Charlottesville Albemarle SPCA, it was huge. They sniffed things and were startled by dogs barking, but made it all the way through. Very, very proud of them. It goes to show how adaptable dogs are when they have food and love and play and a secure home. Yea Sasha and Sadie!

I didn't mention the other 72 times they wouldn't walk. Or that sometimes they would get halfway around the block and then panic and sprint for home. Or that other times if I was walking just Sasha and Blue, I would have to carry Sasha part of the way if she got scared. It helps to restrict yourself to yourself to dogs you can carry if you're going to bring home a shy dog or two. My limit is 50 pounds, but I am strong-ish. I can haul a 50 pound dog for a block with frequent stops.

This entry, though, was totally true: "Sadie and Sasha tolerated having their toenails trimmed and me running the vacuum cleaner. Two huge milestones!"

The two un-socialized, super shy pit bull puppies were now following me everywhere I go in the house. They went from scared to having separation anxiety – do not pass go, do not collect 200 dollars. I would go to get the mail and Sadie would give me a flat tire when I got back in she was so close. It was like have two shadows. They were becoming so curious and comfortable. They still startled easily, but they recovered much more quickly. They just wanted to be with you.

And then the cats even decided to move back in. One other area I liked to brag about on the blog was how good the girls were with our cats: "Official verdict? Good with cats," I wrote early on. "Good" of course is relative, but they didn't eat them, or even try to. Sadie and Sasha understood the rules – the cats were part of the pack and not to be eaten. I even had a photo to prove it. (But the sales pitch, true as it was in our house, came back to haunt me. So much of good dog and cat interaction depends on the cat. The rest depends on vigilance and exercise.)

Skye and Jekyll are our two tabby cats that we got when they were six weeks old from a woman I worked with when we first moved to Virginia. At the time we got them, they were obviously too young to be separated from their mother because they immediately bonded with Thor and Odin. Our big beautiful Boxers look perplexed to have adopted kittens, but they shrugged and let them stay. It was cat heaven in the country. We let them go in and out as they pleased and they took to the country lifestyle.

Skye loves to play with dog toys.

When we moved to the city, we knew we needed a safe street with a big back yard so the cats could still go in and out. We were very solicitous of their needs. They took to Piper all right, but Blue threw them for a loop at first.

Skye and Blue

When Sadie and Sasha exploded into the house, Skye moved outside again. Jekyll hid. Basically I figured they were thinking: "Seriously? Two MORE pit bulls? We barely have tamed the ugly one." But Sadie and Sasha were "good with cats." When Sadie and Sasha looked out the window and saw our two cats on the porch, they totally ignored both - as Rob said, they looked through them. Skye's desire for attention and love and the milk at the bottom of the cereal bowl soon trumped any fear. Plus, she had her earlier success under her belt. It was as if she realized, Sadie and Sasha were great - no aggression whatsoever. Sadie got up and sniffed Skye, but it didn't bother Skye at all. As Sadie and Sasha grew more comfortable, they showed more interest in the cats, which was not ideal. But Skye and Jekyll were nothing if not dog savvy, and we kept the dogs exercised, supervised, and entertained.

Sadie's biggest crime against the cats was that she tried to make Skye's bed into a chew toy. It was enough of a problem when Skye wasn't in it, but it was more serious when she was there. She didn't want to be displaced and fought back. We kept an eye on things, but didn't worry too much about it.

Jekyll on my desk. Yes, that is her look all the time.

Pit bulls and cats don't always go well together, but we were special and careful enough to make it work, I figured. Plus, the girls didn't ever go after the cats; no they just gave a little chase every now and then. I was never going to write that in their blog - no that wasn't "happy" enough. I needed to sell these dogs. That was my job. As well as things were going, we were still running out of energy for this project. And life was intruding: our big swim across the Chesapeake Bay (4.4. miles in rough water) was getting closer, and sleep helps a lot when you are training for an athletic event of that magnitude.

Sasha sniffing Skye and Sadie watching Piper get on the couch.

Saving Sadie and Sasha

Chapter 12 – Halfway Up the Mountain

The first month was a total honeymoon phase, most of the time. The work seemed like play. Rob and I were tickled with our achievements and the dogs' transformation. Success feels good. But we were only halfway up the mountain; we still had to get to the summit and then safely back down. We were tired, and it was getting dark (figuratively speaking). Plus, as the girls' fear lessened, their wants and needs changed. It was good to see them not scared, but once that all-encompassing fear left them, there was a void into which other needs came. Like the need to be dominant and the need to have the Lady resource all to themselves. This was the time to start training, but training is hard when there are multiple dogs in a house and you are just trying to keep them all alive and happy. This transition into the "work" phase was hard for us, and we weren't terribly good at it.

Sadie and Sasha never did anything "wrong" in our home, but their world was opening up and they didn't know how to react to it. They were experimenting with boundaries. Which is what all dogs do, and why shelter life is particularly hard on dogs who need boundaries. In a shelter, dogs don't know what is theirs and what is their neighbor's. This is the source of many problems. While no dog wants to be bad, sometimes we set them up to fail accidentally. I remember a day when I worked at the shelter when there was a dog fight that could have been avoided. I always preached keeping the dogs apart when I trained volunteers, but it was easy to be careless. Two young women were taking out dogs in adjacent kennels. They were chatting with each other and not very focused on the task at hand. And why should they be? The concept of a dog fight wasn't even on their radar. One dog was a large, beautiful male pit bull, and the other was a large, white fluffy female dog. She looked like a Samoyed mixed with a German shepherd. She was kind of feisty and dove toward the male's kennel just as the young woman was opening the door. The pit bull reacted by grabbing the other dog's neck in a defensive gesture.

I could see his eyes as his teeth were latched onto the other dog's neck. They seemed to stare straight into my soul. "I had no choice," he seemed to say. I knew it was already too late for him. Dog aggression in a pit bull meant he would be put down. End of story. That was the policy at the time. But I still tried to break it up, and I was kicking his head to try and get him off of her. I was shocked by the violence of the scene, and by my own capacity for violence. But this time, the violence was directed to stopping further violence. I got him off her, but he knew he was screwed. He knew he had done something wrong, and my heart broke for him. It was only wrong because it was against the rules of the shelter. If he were out in the real world, he would just be defending himself. No dog – or at least no dog I have ever known– wants to be bad. They just want fair and understandable rules and they want everyone to follow them. Life is unfair, though, and in so many ways. All the good and bad stuff is distributed unevenly. This is particularly true when it comes to animals, or any part of nature that relies on man's largesse and his rules.

I had only ever seen two shelters in my life – Atlanta's and Charlottesville's. Then one day towards the end of my tenure at the

CASPCA, we got a call that the shelter in a nearby county needed help. That shelter housed most of its animals outside, and an early and severe cold snap was coming. They weren't prepared. They had to get all their animals inside somehow, but they didn't have enough space. I had instructions to help by bringing two dogs back to our shelter.

I drove our rickety van down the narrow country roads to get to the dark and unmarked shelter. I missed the turn twice. It felt like a scene from a low budget horror movie. (Note to self – always keep a flashlight in purse. A headlamp would be even better.) Anyway, I got there because I finally followed the barking. I got out, met the people involved and had to pick two dogs. Quickly. It was after 9pm. They had to be "easily adoptable" dogs – we had our own tough cases. So no pit bulls or other dominant breeds, no big hounds, no obvious medical cases. There were so many dogs to choose from, though, and the place smelled foul and looked like a Turkish prison. Some of the dogs who had made it inside were in tiny crates filled with excrement. I couldn't stand it. I couldn't stand the power of choice I had, either. But I did not have the luxury of wallowing, and at least I could do something for a few dogs. So I picked myself up by the metaphorical scruff of the neck and told myself to suck it up. I needed to make my choices and get back. After some dithering about the consequences of bringing one too many, I picked three. A small thin tan and white hound, a border collie-ish looking dog, and a non-descript brown and black shaggy dog. All were probably 30-40 pounds. I loaded them into the van with the help of the shelter staff and pointed myself back home. I was emotionally exhausted, and I had an hour drive ahead of me. Then I had to get them settled for the night with food and water and beds.

I couldn't help but imagine how confusing it must be for them to be yanked out of their home, as crappy as it was, thrust into a van, and plopped into new kennels in a new place. I had to name them, too, for our database. They became Lemon, Juno and Scout. Lemon because it was cute, and pale colored hounds are often called lemon hounds. Juno, because I had just seen the movie, and Scout for the heroine in *To Kill A Mockingbird*. Scout (left) and Lemon (right) are pictured below:

The next day, I got a little ribbing for taking three, and for the fact that two of them had heartworm disease but they all settled in and two were up for adoption within a few weeks. (We were able to treat the heartworm.) Scout, though, was very frightened of people. That seemed strange to me, because he was easy to handle at the Dilwyn shelter. But the vets could barely touch him; he was fear aggressive like Sadie and Sasha, but since he wasn't a pit bull, he got a few extra chances. Luckily, he did come out of his shell in a month, but there were a few tense moments.

It made me happy to help them, but I stayed haunted by that shelter for a long time. But that is what you have to do when you're in a rural county and there is no money. Susanne told me they had to live with people just throwing their dogs over the fence when they didn't want them anymore. So.

Everyone lined up to adopt the Michael Vick dogs because they came with a horrible story and it made people feel they were doing something more special than just giving a homeless dog a home. It was like they were making up for Vick's sins to the entire dog world. Good for them. Those sins are still unimaginable to me. But there are millions of dogs with less tragic backgrounds who are nonetheless damaged and need help. And when you can't help them because there aren't enough resources or because they are beyond help, medically or behaviorally, you put them down. You sit with the ones who you cared extra about and cry when their life slips away. But before that, you try and be strong, so they aren't scared. It is your chance to absorb some of their pain and fear. Death is all around, even at the best animal shelters.

In the final equation, *all* dogs ask you to do your best and forgive you when you can't. But troubled dogs? They'll have a beer and a smoke with you and settle into the rocking chair on the porch and say "Oh, man, I've been there too. Let me tell you about the time...." They know they don't fit in. They know they are broken, just like you. We are all broken, some of us just don't try to hide it. Not to belittle the horrors some dogs have survived, but cruelty isn't what makes most dogs troubled or lands them in the shelter. It is simple neglect. People overestimate their capacity. They want the idea of a dog, the love of a dog. But any relationship takes work, particularly when it is between two entirely different species. (Now seems like a good time to add that there are many, many dogs in shelters around the country and world who are emotionally and physically completely healthy. And there are plenty of dogs who come from breeders that are crazier than a jaybird. Just for the record.)

It's easy to spend one evening driving to the country and saving three dogs. What comes after is sometimes the hardest work. I was hoping I hadn't overestimated my capacity for work.

Chapter 13 – Holy Cow! Potential Adopters!

When you can get a dog out of the shelter environment, it is good for everyone. Obviously, it is good for the dog; it allows the shelter to have room for another dog; and it means the dog may get seen by people who would never dream of visiting a shelter for whatever reason. That is why fostering is such an integral part of a shelter being a No-Kill facility, or a life-saving facility, if you prefer that term. But foster homes are not forever homes; if they were, they wouldn't be very good as foster homes. It was time for Sadie and Sasha to take their next steps.

When shelter management officially decided that Sadie and Sasha would be available for adoption, having passed their temperament tests (which we sort of did unofficially at home – I think Susanne just liked the videos I posted), I wrote the following entry on their blog:

> Sasha and Sadie are now available for adoption through the Charlottesville-Albemarle SPCA!! They are still shy with strangers and timid in new situations, but they are amazing, wonderful pets. Even though they are nine months old, because their emotional development was so stunted, they still have a lot of puppy qualities. But they are housebroken, so you get the best of both worlds! Why don't we want to keep them if we love them so much? Because we want to be able to foster more dogs in the future. Plus, our dog Piper is not the world's biggest fan of being one of four. She would prefer being one of one, but she tolerates (and sometimes loves) her brother Blue.

Rob and I celebrated our accomplishment and made ourselves ready to receive a flood of calls and visitors. Oh, the naiveté. In addition to advertising the girls' availability for adoption on my blog, the shelter listed them on their website and on Petfinder, a nationwide pet adoption website. This was how the first call came through. I think it was Ashley who called me saying someone was interested in seeing them and gave me the person's phone number. I nearly did a cartwheel of joy. The only thing stopping me was that I can't actually do a cartwheel. I called the person back, and since he sounded nice, we set up an appointment for him to come visit at lunch so Rob could come home from work and be part of what I hoped would be a new beginning for the girls. Who could resist them after seeing them in person!

At the appointed time, a shiny, black BMW pulls into the cul-de-sac. It wasn't a run of the mill shiny black BMW either, it was one of the giant ones that your dad would drive if your dad was rich and show-off-y. But that's okay, I told myself not to judge. And there is nothing wrong with money; it certainly helps with toy-buying and trips to the vet. Money is good, I repeated. Rich people are nice, too.

Two people got out of the car, a man and a woman, or rather a boy and a girl. They were so young, I wasn't quite sure what to call them. They smiled as Piper barked her head off (good sign) and Blue charged down the steps wagging his tail with the sheer joy of having visitors. Sadie and Sasha were also barking, sporadically.

Our house is on a hill, so when they started up the steps, we were looking down on them. A few steps later, still far from the top, they were looking down on us. They kept coming and getting larger.

They were, in other words, very tall. They could legitimately be called giants. Literally. He played football, and she was a swimmer. Both were well over six feet and not skinny. Imposing. Beautiful and strong and healthy, but very imposing. So we looked up and shook hands. This was not good, though. Timid dogs don't like anyone who shops in the big and tall section.

Before inviting the giants into our home, I put Piper in the bedroom and let Sadie and Sasha outside. I wasn't quite sure how they would act in the house. I thought being outside would give them some freedom and confidence. I was wrong. It gave them a place to run away. I felt so bad for our guests. I led them through the living room and kitchen and straight to the backyard. They wanted to pet the girls – who wouldn't? - but Sadie and Sasha were like "Hell no. They want to kill us." Maybe we should have done a better job of exposing them to a variety of people, but our neighbors are little people. Rob is a big-ish guy at 6 feet and 185, but they still weren't totally sure of him, especially when he stood up suddenly.

Despite the bowl of magic hot dog pieces which we had at the ready, Sadie and Sasha didn't exactly show their charming side. To be more specific, they went to the far corners of the yard, put on their hairy eyeballs and barked whenever we looked at them. I felt badly for the potential adopters but then again, I wasn't sure they were a perfect fit. The dogs would be staying with the guy's mother and her other son, a ten year old. So shouldn't she meet them and decide if she needed two high maintenance dogs, I thought? Maybe Sadie and Sasha sensed my unease and that made everything worse. Rob was even more suspicious, but he enjoyed talking about Sadie and Sasha. The poor girl/woman was tortured by how cute the dogs were, but she was never actually going to be able to lay a finger on one.

Still, I must give the guy credit. He was interested in pit bulls because some of his teammates had them. He could have gone for a puppy, but he looked to adopt, and wasn't put off by their descriptions. Here's what he would have read about Sasha (that I wrote) on the CASPCA website:

Gorgeous Sasha came with her sister Sadie to the SPCA as a nine month old pit bull mix who had never lived anywhere outside of a pen in her owner's backyard. She was terrified of the world and everything in it. After a week in a foster home (with two other dogs and two cats) she has blossomed. Sasha is timid with strangers, but walks well on a leash. Sasha has a huge smile that looks like she's about to sneeze. Sasha likes to curl into your lap. She can be both more timid and more bold than Sadie with some things. Outside on a leash, she is a little nervous when other dogs approach her she needs time to adjust. She's happy go lucky, but startles easily, which is understandable considering her sad background. Forgiving and loving, she is still learning to trust and likes to be given some space to make her own decisions. Sasha loves toys (cardboard boxes work great) and still has a lot of puppy in her. She loves the backyard too, but isn't hyper. She only barks when she has something to say. Add a little more training (with treats, she'll learn the basics quickly) and Sasha will make a terrific dog.

And about Sadie:

Sadie loves her people and dances around like a colt when she is excited. Still a little afraid of wide open spaces and doorways and the barking of other dogs and timid around strangers, Sadie is building up her courage quickly. Curious and a gentle eater, Sadie likes to sleep on her sister or one of her foster siblings or on your lap. She is crate trained and quiet; she kind of keeps an even keel. Sadie does like to wrestle with her sister, but can be happy in a separate room too. She loves to run and romp in the backyard, but she isn't overly energetic. She plays well with her foster sibling dogs. A little patience (not surprising considering her sad background) and some further training (easy because she loves treats) and Sadie will be a fantastic dog!

Seriously, I know I made them sound good, but a kid at a prestigious educational institution such as UVA would have been able to read between the lines, even if he is a football player. (Sorry, don't mean to stereotype football players or jocks of any kind. I married a college athlete and he is very smart. He is also reading this book.) They would clearly have been a lot of work for a college student (or his mom) and he was willing to take time out of his schedule with his girlfriend, go to a stranger's house and look at a pair of crazy dogs. I was impressed, and there was a point a few months later when I even considered calling him back, but I am getting ahead of myself again. We followed his football career the next fall and even kind of cheered for him and the UVA football team despite the fact that Rob is a Texas Longhorn and I am a Tarheel.

Of course, throughout this rather uncomfortable meeting, Blue was utterly charming, wagging his tail and thrusting his head into the new folks' laps. We probably could have gotten him another home, but that option was not on the table. Overall, this was a good learning experience for me. I was surprised at how protective I felt of the girls, how unwilling I was to let them go. Of course, they weren't exactly bounding out of the door either. I realized I would need to be more open to a variety of situations. Okay, I would be better next time. I learned my lesson.

Weeks went by. Helloooooo, next time, where are you?

Chapter 14 – "You Deserve a Break Today"

Whether or not you partake of Mc Donalds™, that old jingle "You deserve a break today!" sure was great. Rob and I desperately needed a break after almost two months of four dogs, and a hamburger wasn't going to cut it. Not even if you added some fries and a shake.

This is sort of my (embarrassing) pattern – go after something with a passion, all gung ho, then burn out. Although I wasn't technically burned out, I was getting close. I felt overwhelmed. I think the letdown of having the first potential adoption visit not go well was more toxic than it should have been. I still adored Sadie and Sasha and they made each day wonderful, but as they were becoming their own dogs, their needs were greater than just love and cuddles and food from me. Was I up to the task? I often hadn't been in the past. I needed a break before I had a breakdown.

Luckily, a break came up in the form of an obligation. No guilt for leaving the girls! My Dad was officially retiring after 51 years of teaching constitutional history at the University of North Carolina at Chapel Hill. There was going to be a big shindig, and I wanted to go. I am an only child – it would have been pretty rotten not to go. So we took Piper and Blue to their regular boarding kennel and dropped Sadie and Sasha back off at the shelter, hoping they might get adopted while we were gone. I mean, there were doing so well with us, why wouldn't they be more open to other people? Okay, so they didn't take a shine to the potential adopters who came to visit, but that was over a week ago, and the girls make so much progress each day. Plus, this wouldn't be on their turf.

It is hard enough to take your dogs to a kennel when you travel; imagine taking them back to the shelter. But we had to. Boarding them with our dogs would have been expensive and maybe not the nicest thing to do to the staff of our kennel. Sadie and Sasha still came with a lot of rules. Plus, it was common practice for foster parents to bring dogs back to the shelter when they travelled. That was one of the perks. Our bank accounts were definitely taking a hit from fostering. Not only did twice as many dogs cost twice as much, but I was working as a freelance writer and wasn't able to take on as much work.

So, we were comfortable with the idea of taking them back to the shelter. The only problem was that no one told Sadie and Sasha that they should be comfortable as well. We were only gone three days, but they apparently thought it was hell. They did not have an easy time, and I guess I should have known better. But sometimes when you want something so much, you ignore that little doubting voice in your head. Hope takes over any other emotion and runs the ship.

The official report was that they would charge the cage at the CASPCA whenever anyone walked by. It's one thing to be shut down, it's another to display obvious aggression, even when it is aggression triggered by fear. They were moved from the adoption floor where they could have been seen, to the back area where dogs with behavior issues are kept. Back to square one.

The worst part was that they didn't even come to me when I went to their kennel. You could see in their eyes that they were scared and confused. They didn't trust me anymore. Two months in a home ruined by three days at the shelter. Luckily, I was armed with hot dogs because I had been warned. I managed to win some of their trust back. But I still had to physically drag them out of the kennel. Getting into the car was a challenge – not a twenty minute challenge like the first time, but a challenge nonetheless. I was desperately hurt and felt terrible about what I had done to them. But, on the ten minute trip home, they started to remember, and once we pulled into the driveway, their tails came up. In the front yard, those tails started to wag. Two minutes later, they were back to their happy selves. So they weren't ruined, but they certainly couldn't go back to a kennel in the shelter. There would be no Plan B. We needed to get them adopted from our home, however long it took.

By the next day, though, Sasha started growling at Blue to keep him out of my office. Some dogs are resource guarders. Other than rawhides, all four of our dogs were good with toys and food. But I had become the resource (was it because I left them?) and Sasha wanted me all to herself. She would share with Sadie, but Blue had to stay away. That was the turning point. I would not see my dogs be miserable. Blue would sit at the threshold of my office, wanting to come in, but bullied into staying out by Sasha's growls. He still had 15 pounds on her, so it was kind of funny in an abstract way. But we live in a concrete world, not an abstract one. The holding pattern had to end. I had to do something. My choice was to stop working in my office, for the time being. A Band-Aid solution.

I was not worried about a fight, just about how bad my poor Blue was feeling. I also felt like a failure. I hadn't fixed Sasha at all, I had just been allowed into her mixed-up head space. Sadie was better mentally, but she was becoming quite the chewer. I think she was bored. We were now almost halfway through May, and our big swim race across the Chesapeake Bay was less than a month off. It was looming in my mind as an impossible feat with so little sleep and so much anxiety.

Jennifer, the Director of Operations at the CASPCA, had given me the option of not bothering with having the girls spayed and leaving it for the adopters to do, but I figured the first few days in a new home would be hard enough for anyone. I couldn't imagine how hard it would be for the girls to adjust to a new home and new people and then go back to the shelter and have your uterus yanked out of your body. So I took them both in for surgery. That bought me another couple of days of peace. The staff vet is amazing, but the volume she has to deal with precludes much fussing over the dogs. It's slice em open, yank out the baby-making bits, stitch em up and ship em out. Poor little things. They had to keep Sadie overnight because she had a more difficult time, but I could take Sasha home. Really, I thought when I saw her? Are you sure she's actually conscious. She looked like the walking dead, still incredible groggy. We brought her home and tried to keep her quiet, but Piper and Blue were far too interested and Sasha wanted to play. But she could only run sideways for a bit until she fell over like a drunkard. So I gave her a pain pill and closed her in the guest room with her bed. I checked on her a bit later and she was out cold. Sadie came through the next day in better shape having spent a quiet night. I had orders to keep both dogs quiet for two weeks. No running and no getting wet. Hah!

Maybe it was the effort of keeping the girls from busting their stiches, but I was exhausted and falling further behind in my work. Sure I could just keep the dogs separated all day, and I tried that some days. I also tried working in coffee shops, but that got expensive, and I am too easily distracted. I had a plan, though, if I could get the CASPCA on board.

Slideshow and poster for Sadie and Sasha at the CASPCA.

Chapter 15– Time for Day Camp at the Shelter

After some high level negotiations with Susanne and Jennifer, I managed to arrange a special "day camp" program for Sadie and Sasha at the shelter. (And by high level negotiations, I mean I begged. The CASPCA occasionally used lobby kennels for shy dogs, but the point of the foster program was to make room for more dogs to be helped. This was the only thing I could think to do to help Sadie and Sasha. And me. Thank God Susanne and Jennifer took pity on me.)

They needed to be seen to be adopted, I argued, and I sensed that if they were in an open pen, they wouldn't charge anyone, unlike their brief, unsuccessful return to the kennel. They were given an open pen, like a baby's play pen, in the front lobby near the cats, right across from the front desk. So the staff could keep an eye on them and Sadie and Sasha could see everything and everyone. They wouldn't feel the anxiety that they so keenly felt in the kennels where they could only see out the front.

Kennels are stressful places for nervous dogs. With a limited field of vision, then can hear things, but they can't see them unless they are right in front of you. I was sure if the dogs could see everything, they would be fine. And they were, if fine equals huddled against each other in a corner of the pen.

Here's how it worked. Every day, a little before noon, when the CASPCA opened, I would drive the dogs to the shelter. At 6pm, when the doors closed, I would return and pick them up, if they hadn't been adopted. Each trip to and from the shelter was a milder version of that original one. Still painful, but quicker.

"I'm so sorry" was what I would say every morning as I took them to the shelter. But they got that primo spot in the lobby as well as two great posters and a video display so visitors could see a slideshow of photos of how they acted in a real home. This would be good for them! And I worked so hard to make it happen! All the exclamation marks in the world didn't scare away the feeling I was a failure. I missed them so much during the day, too.

Sadie in the car. Lip licking is a sign of stress

Others were picking up my slack, though. Kaicee, a front desk employee, made those great posters and Ashley would try and walk them. This was good, I told myself. They needed exposure to other people. I had really done all I could. At the end of each day, they would come home and play in the yard and eat good food and sleep in their fluffy bed. It was the best compromise I could come up with. But it couldn't last forever. Luckily, it didn't have to.

Another poster on their special lobby kennel.

Chapter 16- Adopted! Happy Dance!

The day camp went on for a few weeks, and then it was time for our Chesapeake Bay swim race. Sadie and Sasha would have to stay overnight in one of the back kennels at the CASPCA, and I would have to rely on the staff to bring them to their lobby lodgings every day. The staff was always busy, and I was concerned. Not because they were not good people, but because there was so much to care about, so many special requests. I tried not to think about it.

The 4.4 mile swim managed to take my mind off their plight for a couple of hours. (If you are curious to know more about the swim: http://www.bayswim.com/history.html) It was a rainy, and the water was warm and choppy. Rob and I both made it across – he was as usual almost an hour faster than me - but I was ready to get home almost as soon as I finished. It would be too late to go back and get them when we got home, so I called Ashley to let her know. She said – wait for it – that they had been adopted! Adopted! Even with two left feet, I could do this happy dance!

My stomach dropped with relief and shock. But hold on, I wasn't ready to never see them again! But, this is the happy ending we dreamed about! But I wasn't there to see it! But, but, but! Such a mixed up cocktail of chemicals were shooting through my body. I think Rob and I spent that evening in a semi-comatose state. Ashley reassured me that the woman seemed like a great home, and we were both thrilled that she took them together.

"It's always darkest before the dawn," I think I said, remembering the tough past few weeks, because I usually speak in clichés in moments of high emotional stress. We were both relieved and bereft at the same time. So that is how it ends, I thought. That's all there is. No fireworks, no tearful goodbyes, no waving into the fog....

A few weeks later, after putting our house and lives back in order, we set off on a real vacation, the first in a few years. After such total dog immersion, we noticed with a little bit of guilt how nice it was to be free of dogs for a while. We had a pet sitter stay with Piper and Blue and headed to New York City and then Lake Placid. It was such a joy to have nothing to worry about, other than jellyfish and boats. I had no soapbox, no obligations, no lives depending on me, nothing to protect. It felt great. We did two more swim races – one in Coney Island and one in Mirror Lake.

Rob and I after the Chesapeake Bay Swim.

Both were wonderful, although my finish times were slower that I would have liked. Go figure. But I didn't mind sacrificing a few finishing places. The past few months had been worth it, and it was time to move on. We got home rested and happy to see our dogs.

Everything was back to normal for about a week, when the universe threw us a big curveball. I'll never know if it was completely related to the four dog dynamic in our house for the past two months, but I figured there had to be a connection. While Piper had gained weight in a sort of protest against playing in the back yard when the girls were there, Blue seemed to just take everything in stride, even when Sasha was bossing him around. That is, until the day in early July when we were charged by a little black Scottie and Blue turned into 50 pounds of bite-and-shake. I am always nervous when I see off leash dogs when I have both of my dogs. Piper doesn't care for other dogs, but when I have her alone, I can pick her up. I could not pick up two dogs, and this little black dog was hell bent on chasing us off. I saw it coming from a block away and so did Blue. It all happened so fast, but just as the Scottie reached us, Blue grabbed him by the neck and shook him like a rag doll. I screamed. He wouldn't let go at first and then he did and the stupid Scottie came back at him. I was sure Blue was going to kill that dog. Finally the dog's owner comes running down the street and I start yelling at her to get her dog. I am kicking Blue to try and get him to let go while still holding Piper's leash. Piper has no desire to participate, thank god. Finally, Blue lets go and the dog sensibly scampers away. It was horrible.

Afterwards, my heart rate is about 200, and clearly Blue's is too. I pull him toward home and away from the crazy dog and check him over. He has blood on his lip and a wild look in his eyes. But he is not soaked in blood. I was sure Blue had ripped the other dog apart. He was shaking it so violently. I got home somehow and then realized I had to go back and at least let the woman know Blue has had his shots and offer to pay the vet bills. Even though her dog was loose and attacked us, I felt I needed to do something. I was just so shocked at what Blue did. I didn't know he had that capacity for violence, and there was nothing I could do to stop it. Sure he was provoked, in a way, but what a reaction.

I got back to the woman's house and damn if the little black Scottie dog wasn't at the door barking at me. I figured it would be a bloody lifeless mess. Nope. And the woman apologized to me for her dog saying he could be quite aggressive and territorial.

"But he's not hurt?" I said, still incredulous.

"No, he's fine, and I'm a vet tech," she said. (A vet tech is like a nurse.)

"Okay…"

"I'm sorry again," the woman said.

I got in my car and drove home trying to figure out how Blue could shake that dog so violently and not hurt it. He must have just been sending a message. I told Rob all about it when he got home, but I don't think he quite believed the whole business was as bad as I made it out. Still, he promised to be extra vigilant about loose dogs. Blue had always been so friendly with other dogs. I wondered if his frustrations with Sasha had led to this? Or maybe it was just an isolated incident. Yeah, that was it, I tried to tell myself. Stop being so dramatic.

But it wasn't an isolated incident. For some reason that summer, we had a spate of off leash dogs (despite a LEASH LAW where we live) who decided to charge at the three of us. Piper or I would tense up first, a change in energy that Blue would pick up on immediately. "All right ladies, I got this," Blue would say, turning to make sure Piper and I were behind him. I could almost see him cracking his knuckles and popping his neck to loosen up in the split second he had before the charging dog would arrive.

I had to break up three dog fights with loose dogs before Rob was finally faced with one. He came home with a puncture wound from the other dog. That's it, I decided. I called my old dog trainer Karen Quillen, who thought it was quite reasonable for a leashed dog to attack an unleashed dog who was charging him, but encouraged me to come back to training class so she could observe Blue's interactions with other dogs. Karen always makes me feel better. Luckily, she had a class starting the next week, so off we went the next Wednesday.

We got there early, because I like to be a teacher's pet. Another of my needy, unpleasant qualities. In the lobby of her facility, Karen saw me and came over to say hello. We were chatting a bit and then in walks Sadie. My Sadie. MY *SADIE?* I break down sobbing. Literally. I become a crazy wailing woman. The poor lady at the other end of Sadie's leash is dumbfounded. Sadie is wagging her tail and licking my face.

"Hi Lady! What up? Why are you down there?" Sadie seems to say.

It was like seeing someone return from the dead. I don't mean to be dramatic – although by now, you know I cannot help it - but that is what it was like. Blue and Sadie played happily during class and Karen pronounced Blue fine with other dogs, reassuring me that she would testify on his behalf if he ever caused any damage. I also figured out a work-around: I would walk the dogs separately. On the rare occasions when I break my rule, I carry a small arsenal including an air horn (to startle another dog away), a can of Citronella spray (dogs hate the smell) and a batch of treats.

Sadie's new mom also adopted Sasha, as Ashley told me, but was only bringing one dog to class at a time, which made sense. I was glad to see they were getting some alone time. Plus I am not sure if I could have handled seeing Sasha. I should not have had a favorite, but I did. So sue me. A small sense of unease comes over me, though, when Sadie and Sasha's new owner explains she wants them to be "ambassadors for their breed." This is a common problem for pit bull lovers. They want (or need) their dog to show the world that pit bulls are all awesome. That is a lot of pressure for any dog to bear, much less one with Sadie or Sasha's personality. I told her to call me if she needed anything, hoping she would never have to call.

PART THREE: The "Hail Mary" Road Trip

Chapter 17- Back on Death Row

She didn't call, but, four months later, Jennifer from the CASPCA did.

"They attacked her cat and she brought them back. The cat's okay, but you know what this means."

No, no, no, no, no, no, no, no!

Yes, I knew what this meant. The CASPCA would not adopt them out again because now they could be classified under Virginia law as dangerous dogs and the CASPCA couldn't risk the potential liability. (Of course, as a lawyer, I would say this is not the interpretation I would have made of the law in question, but I had to respect and follow the rules.) I didn't argue. I tried to be professional. Fostering was a *job*, after all. A volunteer job, but a job nonetheless. But something died in me that day that took a years to grow back.

Jennifer let me have time to try and find a rescue group to take them. (Rescue groups are often all-volunteer organizations that use foster homes to "house" their dogs. They are private organizations and often not subject to the same restrictions – real or imagined – as shelters, especially shelters that also serve as city or county pounds. Partnering with rescue groups is a vital part of the No-Kill equation for any animal shelter.) But in Virginia, and everywhere, there are so many pit bulls who have not attacked cats who are waiting for homes. Rescues are full and have waiting lists.

The odds were against me. I was devastated, but I started searching and emailing and calling.

I was also confused. I had trouble believing the story. Sadie and Sasha never attacked our cats. Sure they were interested, but it never went too far. Didn't that count as evidence they weren't going to actually kill a cat? Plus, they didn't actually kill a cat! But I had to play the cards I was dealt.

A week later, I felt I had done everything I could. The rescue groups were full. No one wanted them. Rob and I talked about taking them back, but after what Blue went through, I just didn't think I could. And it took Piper so long to become her old self again, to be even willing to go outside and play. It was as if she had to wait for the backyard to de-contaminate itself. I came up with excuse after excuse. But maybe we could keep them separated in the basement? Isn't any life better than death? Maybe we could take one? Which one? Sadie would have been easier, but Sasha was the one I wanted.

I visited the girls daily. They were being kept in a back kennel, on death row, and looked horrible. Sasha looked red-eyed, like a person who had been crying. They needed help, and I couldn't help them. I was out of options. I had to put my dogs' needs first. I had decided I was willing to let Sadie and Sasha die to protect our dogs and their quality of life. What did that say about me? But, it was only supposed to be for a weekend anyway. I would hold them as they died. I wouldn't quit them at the end; I would live through the horror. Somehow. I told myself this would mean I was not a quitter. But, of course, that is what I was doing – quitting on them. I felt sick.

Chapter 18 -"I'll Drive Them to Colorado"

I could not believe he would put himself through it, but Rob wanted to go to the shelter to say goodbye to Sadie and Sasha. So on the last Saturday in November, we steeled ourselves for an emotionally rocky visit. We took them outside to play together in an enclosed pen and fed them leftover turkey and petted them and just tried to give them a good time. For the last time. They seemed so happy and *normal*, like a regular pair of dogs getting to go outside and romp. They were happy to see us, and happy to be outside. There was nothing wrong with them. Nothing. It was so strange to have to mix the image of them playing happily with what we knew would happen to them in the next few days. They didn't deserve that.

We were leaving the shelter after returning the kennel key to the volunteer office when I saw that Susanne, the executive director, was in her office. She was playing with a puppy. A puppy! Oh, how I needed to pet a puppy. A puppy is full of hope and promise and life. We stuck our heads in.

"How's it going with Sadie and Sasha?" she asked.

"I can't find any place for them," I said, kneeling down and pulling the puppy to my face and kissing its belly.

"Maybe Longmont will take them," she said in the same tone of voice one would say: "I feel like Chinese for lunch." Could she not know she just threw me a lifeline?

"What's Longmont?" I asked, trying to play it cool.

"It's in Colorado. They have a program there." Susanne went on to explain that Aimee Sadler, a dog behavior expert normally based in Southampton Animal Shelter in New York who was working at Longmont Humane Society in Colorado, had come to the CASPCA a few weeks earlier and hosted a dog play group seminar. With the help of a donation from Animal Farm Foundation, Longmont was willing to take two CASPCA pit bulls that Sadler had identified as good candidates into their behavior and rehabilitation program. All the we had to do was get them there. But Susanne only wanted to send one dog of the two they selected as good candidates for their program – Pooch – because she didn't think the other one should make the trip.

"So maybe they'll take three instead of two," she offered casually. "But I just don't know how to get them there."

Why didn't anyone tell me this before I went through this hell? I wanted to scream.

"I'll drive them all to Colorado," I said instead.

"Really?" she said and looked at me for what seemed like a full minute. I think she was evaluating both my seriousness and my capacity to make the trip. She didn't have the time to put everything in motion if I was going to back out. "Okay. I'll make some calls," she said, her decision made. And that was that. No, "are you sure?" No, "gee, it's a long drive." No, "let's try something else." It was life or death and we all knew it. This was Sadie and Sasha's only chance. I looked at Rob, and he smiled, and it was settled.

All the big stuff in life happens like that when you think about it. We dither over which movie to see, but when it comes to sacrificing a week of my life and most of my savings account to save a couple of dogs? It takes me one second to make that decision.

Luck. I never thought I was a person who had it. Now, I figured I just might have used it all up. But that was fine. I was on cloud nine. I felt like I won the lottery. I felt like I was coming out of a tunnel back into the light. I felt like I could breathe.

We had a plan. It was time to move ahead.

Saving Sadie and Sasha

Chapter 19 - What Makes Longmont So Special?

Sadie and Sasha needed to learn how to trust and how to behave in a world that was bigger than our backyard and that was still foreign to them. *I* had to trust that *they* could build *their* capacity to trust at Longmont Humane Society. I planned to drive the girls there with no real idea of what I was getting them into. Trust and faith have never been my strengths. But now they were all I was living on in the way that a person at the bottom of a dark well will grab a rope without worrying too much who is on the other end. All I knew – all I needed to know – was that they would have a chance. They had that chance thanks to Susanne's willingness to call in a few favors and thanks to the Behavior and Rehabilitation program that Aimee Sadler started at Longmont. Susanne basically told me that if Longmont couldn't help Sadie and Sasha, no one could.

This program – indeed any kind of training program for shelter dogs - takes a lot of money because it takes a lot of well-trained people. Those people, in turn, need a salary. Most shelters, even the best ones, operate on a shoestring and cannot afford enough help.

The CASPCA didn't have these kinds of resources, but they had created a great and willing group of foster parents. Fostering saves lives just like a good behavior program does. It just is more de-centralized and more is left up to the individuals involved. That is neither good nor bad in principle, just different. Fostering, at least with me, just was not enough for Sadie and Sasha.

Longmont did have these resources. It was as if Sadie and Sasha had been diagnosed with cancer and now had the chance to go to the best hospital in the world. But instead of an operation, they would get play groups. Other well-balanced dogs would serve as their "doctors" – more like psychologists and bouncers, if needed - because they could speak their language.

"Play groups are a fundamental piece of the puzzle," Sadler says. I knew Sadie and Sasha played well with Blue, so I wasn't sending them someplace where they would be expected to exhibit skills they didn't have. I was excited to think of them frolicking with other dogs and people. At Longmont, there are no different rules for pit bulls, or other dominant breeds, either. "Pit bulls are not innately more aggressive," Sadler says. "That is why dog fighters have so many failures. I think it's like human beings – maybe only five percent of all dogs [or humans] are truly dangerous," she offers. That didn't mean Sadie and Sasha would get special treatment, just that they wouldn't have to meet any different standards just because they were (or looked like) pit bulls.

When I agreed to drive Sadie and Sasha to Longmont, I knew none of the details of Longmont's program. After I got back and was writing this book, I wanted to know more. So, after an email request, Sadler put me in touch with Rhea Moriarty, the director of behavior programs at Longmont. Moriarty explained why the staff at Longmont is more tolerant of difficult behaviors in the shelter and willing to adopt out animals with some imperfect behaviors whether or not they are dominant breeds. The answer is science: "We have a year's worth of data that shows of resource guarders who guard food or toys at the shelter, only 5-10% exhibit that behavior at home. In other words, dogs behave differently in a shelter than at home, and that is okay."

Their goal is to support the animal and adoptive family once the dog is in the home. "Don't spend all your financial resources and staff time and energy trying to predict the dog's behavior – and then kill the dog," she says, "when you don't even really know what he or she would be like in the right home." Sadler, when I spoke with her later, put it more bluntly speaking of both Longmont and Southampton: "We don't kill animals just in case."

"I'm always willing to try," says Moriarty. "We can't control the animal once it leaves us, nor can we control the humans. But we don't euthanize just in case," she says, echoing Sadler. In a larger sense, Moriarty says, "we need to remind people that dogs are dogs. Animals can't reason and they aren't children. Some behaviors and are natural and can't be reasoned with. Sometimes you just need to leave the dog alone when it eats. We always keep the community and its safety in mind, though," Moriarty adds, "and there are three things we can't work with even in our behavior program:

1) Offensive aggression to people (attacking when there are other options like escape).

2) Unpredictable aggression (if they can't figure out a trigger) and

3) Uninterruptable drive (dog must defer to a human between it and a cat)."

Well, I knew Sadie and Sasha were interruptible, and I knew they were not offensively aggressive. In fact, Sadie got distracted so often, I am surprised she ever got anything accomplished. Not that her "to do" list was long or difficult – I believe nap, eat, run, and play were the activities that dominated her list. Oh, and moving shoes and chewing the rocking chair. Still, not highly complex. Sasha was more self-directed, but she also always needed to know where I was and what I was doing. Nor were they unpredictable. They were very predictable. I didn't know anything about Pooch, but Susanne thought he was a good candidate, and that was good enough for me.

Sadie and Sasha's new temporary home wasn't going to be free, though. If so, everyone would be driving their animals to Longmont and there would be no space. "You have to save space to deal with your community's animals," Sadler says. (Longmont was an open admission shelter, meaning by contract with their community they had to take any stray or surrendered animal that came through their doors.) The fee for Sade and Sasha and Pooch was $500 each. The number is based on the cost per day of caring for and working with an animal multiplied by the average length of stay. "You need money to do the work. It's a good business model to get paid for what you do," Sadler explains.

Regarding money, Animal Farm Foundation's role can't be overstated. They were paying the "tuition" for two dogs which is what opened the door for this whole road trip. They couldn't cover a third – no non-profit has unlimited resources – but Susanne and Jennifer and some other CASPCA staff and volunteers chipped in. People on miniscue salaries who have to see dogs be unlucky so much of the time were willing to pay good money so Sadie and Sasha could get a shot. I felt honored on my behalf and on theirs. The expression "It takes a village" doesn't just apply to raising children. With so many people in my corner, and in Sadie and Sasha's corner, I had the easy part. All I had to do was pay for gas and motels, hope fro good weather and clear my calendar.

Saving Sadie and Sasha

Chapter 20 – Getting a Co-Pilot and a Hitchhiker

All I had to do now was get them to this great place where there were people who could help them. This great place that was over 1,700 miles away in the middle of winter. Well, it is undoubtedly always 1,700 miles away from Charlottesville, but those miles are feeling extra-long given the looming threat of snow. It is December, after all. I don't like to drive in snow, particularly not with precious cargo. Turn into the skid, they said in my drivers' education class. Really? I could never get that to make sense in my head, and, living all of my life in the South, I never got to practice.

It did not help that I am a champion worrier. I don't want to be, but I am. And not just about snow and whether there were even enough peanut M&Ms in the universe for a 3,400 mile road trip. Six days, in December, in the *middle of the country*. I am kind of fond of the coasts; the middle of the country is foreign land to me. Big square states with rodeos and pick-ups and people who surely would hate pit bulls. In addition to snow and ice, I envisioned car trouble and lunatics and policemen with guns and exhaustion and dog fights in the car and being turned away from motels and giving up in the middle of Kansas in a pile of tears.

I tried to see if airlines would fly them. I mean what a great story for the holidays! Apparently, I am neither a salesman nor a fundraiser. I called around, went to travel agents, even called a Colorado beer company who had just started distributing their delicious wares in Virginia. Nope. Nothing. Someone finally told me it would be too cold to fly them as cargo in December. Ah, of course. Once that was off the table, I realized what a stupid idea it was. Two scared girls travelling in cargo and then waiting on the tarmac in the snow (this was how I envisioned it) for a stranger to come and get them? It wouldn't exactly be setting them up for success. And it might just be the stressor that finally broke them. No. Driving was the only option. I had to calm down and put on my big girl pants, and finish what I started. Keeping them now seemed like the easier option.

It is funny, people were either amazed or indifferent when they heard about my plans. When you tell people you are driving three pit bulls to Colorado, their reaction tells you a lot about them. From "regular" people I heard: "What the hell? You're crazy." From "shelter" people I heard some version of: "Oh, that reminds me of the time I drove 24 puppies from Houston to Washington. Without stopping." People involved in animal rescue have all paid their travellin' dues. People on the "outside" think you are nuts.

Speaking of on the outside, I made the mistake of telling my mother what I was planning. My mother is 80-ish and I am her only child. What was I thinking? She was sure we would be attacked at a rest stop. Just because I was also a little afraid of that didn't mean I was going to give in. "Really, Mom? With three pit bulls? That would be one gutsy attacker." I wouldn't have told her if she and my dad hadn't been in my home the week before for a short visit and asked how Sadie and Sasha were doing. My parents, whose memories are going and who nap a lot, decided to ask the one question I didn't want to answer. I could not lie, though, I stink at it, so I told her. I also told her it would be fine and that MY HUSBAND DIDN'T MIND ME GOING. "If he thinks I can do it, I probably can. He knows me a bit better that you since I haven't lived with you MOM SINCE I WAS 17!" Sorry, my mom makes me yell. She tried to throw money at the problem saying she would pay to fly them, but I explained how that wouldn't work. Money is nice, but it wouldn't really fix this particular transportation problem. Poor mom, though, her only way to participate was to worry. I did not need another worrier; I had that covered. So we agreed to disagree.

Once the options were gone and Mom was taken care of, I started getting fired up. It was a relief to be able to do something. Plus, I had decided that this trip was just like a big swim. I was an endurance athlete – what was this trip other than an endurance challenge? I could do it. I just needed to pick a date and go.

In the middle of the date-picking process, my friend Stacey called. I told her what was going on. She said. "Oh, maybe I'll go!" My first reaction was: "Are you nuts?" I wasn't even sure I wanted another person along, even my wonderful friend Stacey, because all my mental preparation involved just me. Changing my mind is like turning a giant tanker in the open ocean – it takes a while. We talked, and we both agreed to think about it. I am not going to divulge Stacey's personal demons, but suffice it to say she has a scar on her face from a beloved dog of her's – and she wanted to avoid the Christmas holiday season. Plus, Stacey is a landscape photographer and she said she had never photographed the middle of the country. She made it sound like I was doing her a favor. Still, I wanted to do this alone.

I came to my senses when I realized it would be much safer FOR THE DOGS to have an extra pair of hands along. So I decided it would be great if she came along. Luckily, Stacey decided the same thing. Although six days in a car with someone I usually just see every month or so? Sure I liked Stacey and she liked me, but would we still like each other after this ordeal? I don't have many friends. I didn't really want to lose this one.

Rob loved the idea of me having a co-pilot. Stacey couldn't leave when I wanted to, so we had to wait an extra two days. That was fine with both shelters, so I started getting ready. Leashes, bowls, food, Benadryl to help the dogs relax (yes, its off–label, but everyone does it) energy drinks for me, the afore-mentioned peanut M & Ms, herbal calming drops for the dogs, lots of blankets and towels, first aid for us and the dogs, ice-scraper, CDs, and oh yeah, some clothes for me. And two dog crates. The dogs couldn't exactly roam around free.

I decided Sadie and Sasha would have to share a crate because Rob's car – a Honda Element – could only fit two crates. (Yes I was taking my husband's car. It was much bigger than mine and handled better in bad weather. Susanne offered me the CASPCA van which is certainly bigger, but I had driven it before and I didn't think it was up to the challenge, to put it mildly.) But which crates? Plastic sided ones or wire ones? I was terrified the dogs would cage fight in such a small space, but wire crates were the only ones that fit and still gave the dogs enough room. Sadie and Sasha were each about 40 pounds now and Pooch was at least 60. I got big pieces of cardboard and sheets to put between and over the wire crates to keep them from seeing each other and getting riled up. I had seen dogs bite each other through a cage.

Now I needed a route and places to stay. Places to stay that took dogs. "Don't tell 'em you have three dogs and don't tell 'em you have pit bulls," Susanne advised. That was good advice; I can be honest to a fault. I got my maps from AAA and looked for towns about the right distance apart and started searching the Internet for motels. I picked the cheap places near the highways, and no one asked how many dogs I had or what kind they had when I called to reserve. For all they knew, I had one Cocker Spaniel.

I had my plan; now all I had to do was execute.

Saving Sadie and Sasha

Me and my friend and co-pilot, Stacey with Rob's Honda Element. You can see Sadie and Sasha in their crate in the backseat. I was trying to look confident for Stacey. I realize I just look goofy.

Chapter 21 - 16 Legs off to Louisville

Sixteen legs? Two humans plus three dogs = 16 legs. Stacey said we needed a name for the iPhone album for the photos she was taking. So 16 legs it was. It said everything we were feeling – that we were one organism heading west, our fates bound together, sealed off from the rest of the world for this journey.

We had everything we needed, at least as best as I could anticipate. The giant bag of peanut M & Ms. Check. Food and water for the dogs. Check. Route figured out. Check. Life put on hold for a week. Two big dog crates. Check. Well, barely. Sadie and Sasha's crate ended up sideways behind our seats which were pushed all the way up. I had to drive with my knees almost touching my chin. Rob was worried about my back, and for good reason, but I could not do anything about the set-up. I wanted the girls close to me so I could intervene in case they got into a tussle. I was worried about re-directed frustration, which can happen in tight quarters when animals are unhappy. It can also happen in any relationship. You know when your boss was a pain and you come home from work and yell at your husband? Like that but with teeth.

I said goodbye to Rob in the morning as he went to work. At noon, on December 12, 2011, said goodbye to Piper and Blue and headed to the CASPCA to load three dogs. I managed this with only one flesh wound. To me. I cut my arm as I was shifting Pooch's crate around. At 1pm, I drove to Stacey's house and she and her partner John were in the driveway to meet me.

There was no time for dillydallying. We had nine hours of driving before our motel. We loaded snacks, Stacey's camera bag

Sadie and Sasha in the crate. Nervous.

and clothes and we were off. It was a nice day and no one was barking. Rested and full of optimism and the energy that comes from beginning anything, I drove west on I-64 to where it joined with I-81 in Staunton, Virginia. Exiting at Lexington, Virginia where I-64 separated from I-81, I noticed an odor. I pulled off the highway, and sure enough, we had barf. At least we got it out of the way early.

I think it was Sadie. She looked fine, and after cleaning it up, I made the executive decision not to feed the dogs breakfast from here on. Not only to save my time and energy from cleaning it up, but for their sakes too. No one, human or animal, likes to barf, I figured. It must have been nerves. Sadie and Sasha had been in the car before, lots of times, but for short trips. For all Sadie knew, two hours into the trip, she was being driven off the edge of the earth.

So, back on the road with the windows open for fresh air even though it was cold, we headed into West Virginia and promptly saw a car fire (above) which Stacey had to photograph. Hopefully it wasn't a bad omen. I mean, how does a car just catch on fire? Luckily, I was still driving. She took over for a shift after the car fire, but we soon figured out she was a better photographer and iPhone checker than driver. It was good to have clearly defined roles.

The Element had a small gas tank, so we had to stop about every three hours for gas. We would let the dogs out to have water and a couple of dog biscuits and a pee, and then we would use the restroom ourselves. We got these stops down to about 25 minutes. For all we had to accomplish, I thought that was pretty good. Sometimes the girls didn't want to get out, and I couldn't bring

*Pooch in the back of the Element at Mile 0 in
John and Stacey's driveway.*

myself to haul them out of their crates. I hoped they had iron bladders. We didn't stop for dinner because we needed to make it to the motel. We just ate snacks and cheese sandwiches I had packed.

Chapter 22 – The First Night and the Next Day

A poorly marked detour around a bridge across the Ohio River that was closed due to epic flooding didn't make it easy, but we finally got to the motel at 10pm. Unloading, walking, and feeding three stressed but extremely curious dogs was the next step. Considering it took a long time and a lot of planning to get them all in there, all of a sudden I wasn't totally sure I wanted to get them out. Maybe we could drive straight on through? At the moment, that seemed easier.

The motel was on the west side of Louisville, actually in Georgetown, Indiana. When we pulled in, after the disastrous detour, a very nice woman checked us in. We had a great room on the first floor near an exit so we could get the dogs in and out easily. And it was around the back. Perfect.

Now, we had three dogs and two crates and two people. What if I had been stupid enough to do this alone? As it was, since I hadn't quite worked out the physics of how to manage everyone. I stood in the parking lot for a while, flummoxed. But not crying. A small, but crucial, victory. Stacey was willing to do anything to help, but she was gracious enough to let me take the lead. That was good for our relationship, but bad for my frozen brain. After a minute, I snapped out of it, got Pooch out of his crate, and gave him to Stacey. I knew Pooch wasn't going to bolt like Sadie and Sasha, but I didn't know much else about him. I found out quickly that he quite liked to be lifted out of the car and down to the ground. That's fine, Pooch, even though you are sixty pounds, I'm glad for the exercise. Stacey jogged with him while I took his crate inside. Next, I grabbed our luggage and the dogs' luggage. It took four trips to get everything but Sadie and Sasha and their crate inside. They were looking at me from inside the car with a combination of excitement and bewilderment.

Stacey took Pooch inside, and I got his food ready. I think once he got his dinner, Pooch realized it would all be okay, somehow. Dogs are forgiving like that; better late than never, they figure. I went back out into the cold to get Sadie and Sasha and then spent the next forty minutes trying to get them to pee. They were too nervous and happy to be in any hurry about it. I felt I could hear their thoughts:

Wait, we've never smelled anything this far west before! Hold on, we can't even think about peeing until we understand where we are!

Eventually, they both peed and Sadie pooped. One for two is good enough in my book. So I knocked on the door with the dogs and Stacey executed our pre-arranged plan. I felt like a lookout giving the clue to the ringleader. She put Pooch in the bathroom with his toy so Sadie and Sasha could eat dinner and explore the room. Then I went back out for the girls' crate. When finally got everything and everyone into the room, it looked like the Element had exploded.

All fed and watered for the night, I put the girls in their crate and let Pooch out. I gave him the toy I got especially for him and he held on to it the way a child would a teddy bear. He was happy but wary and confused.

Pooch with his new toy in Georgetown, Indiana.

"Lady, I'm not sure why we're here, but thank you for my toy." He didn't chew it, he sort of cradled and kissed it. It was probably the only familiar thing he had seen in a while.

Sasha couldn't quite take the attention Pooch was getting and started to cry. Sasha's crying was not a pleasant sound. So we put Pooch in his crate and let the girls out. They proceeded to jump on the bed. Yes, we had one bed for the two of us, but since it was midnight, it didn't matter much. After a few reassuring and calming pats, I put the wriggling girls in their crate and we hit the sack. Luckily, neither Stacey nor I are large or smelly or have too many issues. So, we settled in. Maybe we brushed our teeth, but I doubt it. According to MapQuest™, we had 867.91 miles, 13 hours and six minutes of driving ahead of us to get to Colby, Kansas, our next stop. I was a little intimidated. It had sounded possible at the AAA office.

First night in Georgetown, Indiana. Dogs are all nestled in.

The next morning, we got up at 4am thanks to Sasha. It seemed particularly dark. Sasha actually woke up at 3 am, and I tried to quiet her for an hour, then gave up. The Benadryl did not work one whit. Or maybe I forgot to give it to the dogs. Getting up so early made me nervous about falling asleep and having a car accident. I added that worry to the ever-present one of being stopped by the police and having the dogs erupt in a frenzy of teeth and growls that would end with bloodshed. I don't know where I got this bottomless capacity for worry from. Oh wait, thanks Mom! But I plunged forward, because once the gun goes off to start the race, you don't stop until the end or until you collapse.

Stacey was game for starting the day. It was better than pretending to sleep and not sleeping. Adrenaline is a powerful thing. Sasha was so happy to get her way that it was infectious. "You're up," she danced! "Let's play!" When I let the girls out of their crate, she and Sadie almost got stuck like the Three Stooges trying to go through the opening. When it was his turn, Pooch was happy but cautious and confused. And I bet he was tired. It was 4 am after all. So we showered just enough to wake ourselves up, not enough to get really clean because who was going to see or smell us? We walked the dogs but didn't feed them as we were mindful of Sadie's tummy issue and remembered that we had fed them giant dinners only five hours earlier. They would get a few treats throughout the day, I told myself. I felt so guilty, but it was temporary.

We reversed the unloading game from last night and managed to fit everything back into the Element. Not quite as neatly, but go figure, right? I was just happy I could shut the hatch. We were on the road at 5:30 and happy about our early start. The sun was just starting to make the sky pink.

Soon we were both even happier to see a brightly lit McDonalds™ on the on-ramp to the highway.

"Coffeeeeeee" we both said, knowing we couldn't get very far without it. I had my emergency energy drink, but just like you're not supposed to try anything new before a race that you haven't tested in practice, I was nervous about ingesting all those weird chemicals on the road when I didn't know how I would respond. (This was by far the most important "race" I had ever entered, so I wanted to be able to finish without falling apart.) Shoot, I figured my head would explode from the taurine or whatever was in them. It was only for emergency, when the risk of my heart exploding was overshadowed by the risk, say, of running off the road. McDonalds coffee was a much safer bet.

It was too early for breakfast, no, we'd save that for the second McDonald's stop of the morning. For someone who loves vegetables and healthy eating, it took less than a day to realize how useful *fast* food can be.

Chapter 23– Now We Are in Kansas

This was the big day of driving. Boy did it make me grateful for our lovely interstate system that drained the rain from the roads quite well. We were aiming for Colby, Kansas, four states away. Indiana and Illinois were kind of a blur, except for the WalMart™.

Driving somewhere in the Midwest. Day.2

It's funny how I can be all high and mighty about how Wal Mart does this and that wrong, but yank me out of my element, and I can be real happy to see one. Same with Starbucks™. It is hard to shop local when you are not at home and in a hurry. A woman on a mission is happy to see a chain store. Principles give way to practicality every time for me. The WalMart parking lot was where Pooch came out of his shell, and he and Stacey started to bond a little. And inside the WalMart was where Stacey got her iPhone adapter so we wouldn't lose juice during our ridiculously long day in the car. We were saved!

The rain started at about six am and continued through most of the day. It was light at least, and Stacey kept saying it would end soon. That ended up being both irritating and hope-inducing at the same time. But not as irritating as the Element's windshield wipers which squeaked. It wasn't raining hard enough to keep them quiet, which was good for driving and bad for the eardrums.

I don't really remember much else about the day of driving, except that it was very much like a long distance swim. You get in the water and you swim until you get to the other side. No need to think about whether or not you are tired, because you can't stop until your feet hit land on the other shore. If you stop, you drown. (Well, not really. You get on the support boat.)

Stacey and Pooch in an Indiana WalMart parking lot.

The St. Louis Arch was pretty special, but beyond that, Missouri made as little imprint on my memory as did Illinois and Indiana. This is probably because we got up at 4 am.

Crossing into Kansas was exciting because it was the last state before Colorado. I had thought Kansas would be flat. I was wrong. We apparently drove on the border of the glaciated region and the *osage questas*, through the middle of the flint hills, the smoky hills and the high plains, in that order. It was lovely. My friend Janice had recommended a bunch of places to see and enjoy along I-70, but we weren't in the mood for sightseeing. We did stop in Salina (on the border of the flint hills and the smokey hills) to check out her veggie café recommendation. Since yesterday, we'd eaten an egg biscuit, a cheese sandwich that I packed, peanut M & Ms, celery, apples, yogurt covered pretzels and granola.

Our first bit of bad luck was that the café was only open Thursdays through Sundays. It was Tuesday. I really wanted a yummy dinner, but not bad enough to wait two days for it. It was hard to readjust. But we found a sandwich shop and had a passable dinner for $11. For two people. This was our first non-car meal. I was so nervous leaving the dogs in the car. I ran out to check on them four times, and each time they all looked at me, like "what? Why are you so panicked? You're stressing me out!" Dogs adapt better than people sometimes. And I think Pooch was keeping the girls calm.

In addition to the constant rain, Kansas brought us car trouble and a 75 mile an hour speed limit. As Rob wrote when he saw Stacey's photo of the sign on Facebook: "Does the Element even go that fast?" "Just barely" was my answer. I was keeping it at 73 and since traffic was light, no one seemed to mind. Facebook updates and photography kept whoever wasn't driving (usually Stacey) occupied during the long day. Worrying about gas (the Element was getting about 12 miles to the gallon and on a twelve gallon tank…well, let's just say that in rural Kansas, gas stations are about 144 miles apart) and the check engine light kept our minds churning once it got dark.

We still had 200 miles of driving to go after dinner, and few towns between where we were and where we needed to get to. I thought the bad gas mileage might be due to the air pressure in the tires, but of course my (meaning Rob's) tire pressure gauge was faulty. And the first gas station we stopped at didn't even have air. The nice older woman tried to direct me to a co-op a few miles down the road, but I couldn't follow her instructions under the best of circumstances. After being up for fourteen hours, I had no chance. I stopped her from drawing me a map. And she looked worried. "Good luck!" she called after us. She seemed sincerely worried, which was sweet and helped somehow. When someone else takes part of your burden, it does lighten your load.

We made it to Colby, Kansas on fumes at around 9:30pm and I have never been gladder to see a truck stop motel in my entire life. It was a pretty darn fancy truck stop, too. You could see the lights from the truck stop a mile down the highway. They could charge admission to this truck stop. It could be Disney, Kansas. Or Las Vegas, Kansas. Even the dogs seemed to like the place more than the first one. It was certainly more lively. We were apparently the last check-in, according to the rather irritated clerk. So sorry, I thought. I'll try to hurry the next time I drive through FOUR GIANT STATES. We did the whole unloading, walking and feeding thing in the six inches of old snow. I still felt extremely lucky we hadn't faced any snow actually falling.

The unloading process went a little smoother since there were always a couple of what I assumed to be truckers outside the door and they held it open for me as I lugged the crates in and out. It is much easier to carry large things into a motel when you do not also have to open the door with your foot. My new trucker friends did seem a little confused about what I was doing, but they didn't pepper me with questions. Actually, they didn't speak at all. Nor did they – or anyone – seem to count dogs or be perturbed by their breed.

Sadie in Colby, Kansas

The dogs loved the snow and peed and pooped much quicker. They seemed to have figured out the rhythm of life. Dogs do this far better than we do, I think. Maybe it is because they don't have much time to waste; their lifespans are so short. As soon as something is repeated, it becomes routine, and they know what to expect. When it was Sadie and Sasha's turn to be free in the room, they enjoyed jumping from bed to bed before curling up in my arms. Yes, this room had two beds!

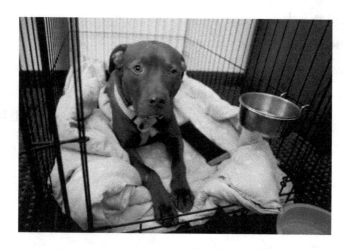

Pooch, looking relaxed and a bit resigned.

Pooch was happy too when it was his turn to explore. He wanted to say hi to the girls, but Sasha would have none of it. So he put himself back in his crate, all by himself. For a tough dog whose reputation was that he played too rough with other dogs, he was whupped by a little girl pit's single snarl even when she was in a cage. I am guessing he was still probably unsure of himself and his place in the pack. Blue took a while to become our dog. And Pooch had the same look. It said: "This seems nice, but I'm not taking it to the bank yet." I'm sure he could sense the bond that Sadie and Sasha and I had. He was the odd dog out, and it kept him on his best behavior.

With all that said, the dogs really were amazing. Except for Sasha's tendency to be an early riser – which you can't really hold against her – they were perfect road trip companions. It was strange. The dogs were truly so easy on this unending day of driving that we figured they should be adopted out to long-haul truckers or anyone who drove for a living and wanted a little companionship. Night number two brought almost a full seven hours of sleep. Unbelievable.

We could see the finish line, and it looked lovely.

Me and Sadie and Sasha, on the bed in Colby, Kansas.

Chapter 24 - D-Day at Longmont

It always helps to have a cheering section. Through Stacey's photos and updates on Facebook, we knew we had people rooting for us at home. It made us feel even more sure of what we were doing, and determined to not only make the trip successful, but make it as fun as possible, a thought that had never entered my mind in the beginning.

After breakfast in Colby, we only had five hours of driving to go. An hour into it, we could see the Rocky Mountains, and the 75 mph sign just wasn't so scary anymore, especially because the roads really were this empty.

We both started to feel the weight of the approaching ending. Although we had only been our "pack" for a little over 48 hours, it was an intense 48 hours. Dogs and travelling both require you to be so fully present, the rest of the world just drops away, Facebook or no Facebook. Facebook was actually our only connection to our prior lives. Without it, we may have become even more unmoored. Getting close to the end was exciting, but it also created an odd feeling of impending loss. It was like wanting something really badly and then getting it and finding out it wasn't what you wanted.

Stacey and I joked about continuing to drive, maybe even heading to Alaska. A part of each of us didn't want this trip to end. The fact it was going so well made us both feel needed. But we carried on. A quick stop in Flagler, Colorado for more gas and a walk for the dogs presented an opportunity for Stacey to take a couple of great photos of train tracks. Stacey bought the Element a new tire gauge so I could breathe easier. The tires had perfect air pressure.

The map made the last leg look easy – all we had to do was head north of Denver and make a couple of turns to get to Longmont Humane Society - but we got lost anyway. We also got lost on the way out, but I'm getting ahead of myself again.

The Longmont facility was part of the state fairgrounds with only a fairly small, well camouflaged sign. We found it, though and although it was a lovely facility, you could just feel the dogs thinking: "1,700 miles to get back where we started?" Getting to the end was both satisfying and horrible. Leaving them seemed impossible. The dogs didn't want us to leave either. It was heartbreaking and utterly awful. We were unprepared for this. Even Pooch was unhappy.

"Seriously? I thought things were going so well?" his big brown eyes said.

Stacey walked Pooch as I found my contact person at Longmont. Then I walked Sadie and Sasha. They were panicked, darting to the end of their leashes in any direction, and I felt awful. We quickly got them settled into their kennels which were in a quiet area reserved for new arrivals and Behavior Program dogs. The girls had adjoining kennels, and the staff opened the door between so they could be with each other as they adjusted. Pooch had the kennel next door. I left his toy with him. It was the least I could do, and it felt so ridiculous.

I cried, Stacey cried, and we had to leave soon or something in me would break. The staff also didn't really need us hanging around crying and stressing out the dogs. I was confident this was the place where the girls had a shot, but I also knew they wanted to be with me. I was trying so hard, though, not to be *that person*. Sure I was bringing my favorite dogs, but everyone there at the shelter already had their favorite dogs. I was told to feel free to call, but that I could also check the website to see when (if) the girls and Pooch would be available for adoption. Ah, the magic Internet. I could keep up without interfering. Perfect. I signed the papers making the transfer official and got my copies to bring back to the CASPCA. They were not mine anymore, not that they ever had been. But at least they were close. There was nothing I could do for them anymore, other than hope and cyber-stalk them. It felt so permanent.

Stacey called this photo "Mission Accomplished."
I call it "Living with Ghosts."
The photo is of us – I am carrying the dogs' empty harnesses.

We went for a long walk before we got back in the car. I just couldn't bring myself to leave right away. But it was time to be practical. I had no real right to mourn, and we needed to eat something and start the trip back.

We found a Panera's™ and had a late lunch at about 3pm, with vegetables! I think that was mountain time, but I'm not sure. We had been through so many time zones so quickly that I was a little confused.

I decided that, even though it would eat up more time, since we were near a real city we should get the car checked out. Stacey's iPhone came in handy again. We found and stopped at an Auto Zone™. Because I might have mentioned we just drove 1,700 miles to bring three pit bulls to Longmont, the guy who helped us shared his pit bull story. He rescued a pit bull after a hurricane in Houston (he can say rescued because he literally did that). "Best dog I ever had," he said. We shared stories and felt a little better. There would of course be people here who would fall in love with Sadie and Sasha and Pooch. It would be okay.

It turned out the check engine light was telling us we were getting bad gas mileage thanks to a busted O2 sensor. Once I figured out thanks to a phone call with the nice woman at Mile High Honda, that the car engine wouldn't blow up and no, it couldn't be fixed this afternoon – it was already 5pm – we planned to head back for the highway. Luckily next to the Auto Zone was a beer store, so we got a couple of six packs first. We just weren't going to make it through this day without a beer or two at the end.

We pointed the Element to Hayes, Kansas and made good time, after getting lost again. Somehow, the roads around Denver were too much for our addled brains. We enjoyed a stop at the Colorado gift shop in Kanorado (best town name ever) where Stacey did her Christmas shopping for her niece and nephew. We almost took the six-foot tall stuffed black bear from the gift shop with us because we were so lonely. I think the nice man said it was only $2,000. We showed restraint, somehow. Once it got dark, the sky filled with shooting stars. Stacey counted thirteen. We pulled into our motel at 11:30 utterly spent.

PART FOUR: Home, Alone

Chapter 25 - Hayes to Hannibal and Home

Stacey and I woke up hungover and deservedly so. I don't recommend two beers on an empty stomach after a couple of hours of crying. The physical pain did make us forget about the emotional pain, though, so if that is your goal, I guess I do recommend it.

We were truly headed home. I desperately need to see my dogs and Rob; they felt like the only things that would heal the emptiness of leaving the girls at Longmont. We took a slight detour, though, to visit some friends in Hannibal, Missouri. One, it would save us some money on a hotel. Two, they would cook real food for us! Three, I was a huge fan of my friends' art work and planned to pick up a piece for Rob, speaking of Christmas shopping. Four, we could tell them our story. The story was practically bursting at the seams to get out. So, after the now routine egg biscuit and coffee, we set out for Hannibal. (The McDonalds in Hayes had gingham curtains, by the way. I had never realized there was such regional variety in McDonalds. I got quite an education.)

Since we had twelve hours to do nine hours-worth of driving, thanks to the time change, I asked Stacey to look for a park on her magic iPhone. I needed a real walk. (By the way, it only took Rob and me a month after I got back to finally pony up the dough to get our own iPhones. That is one handy little gadget when you are far from home.) She found one and we had a lovely time until I realized there was no one around and we were in the wilds of Missouri without dogs for company / protection.

"We're going to get our heads chopped off," I said to Stacey. "You think," she answered, cocking her head reminding me of Sadie.

We decided to hightail it back to the car. After our little jog, we got back on the road and arrived at Joachim and Janice's house in Hannibal at about 6:30pm. It felt like another oasis, better even than the Colby, Kansas truck stop. It did not feel like we had been pushing so hard until we arrived at a peaceful home. I almost melted. Janice fixed us dinner and breakfast with produce from their garden. It was positively restorative.

Joachim had bought this old house in Mark Twain's hometown for a song and had been fixing it up over the years. He did everything himself: plumbing, roof, interior re-configuration, kitchen, garden, everything. He is that kind of artist. And Janice makes gorgeous jewelry. They are such contained, happy people who are content right where they are. It was an antidote to driving

and fixing things. A reward. Another reward was the best night's sleep I had had in years on the floor in Joachim's studio.

And speaking of his studio, I brought home this wonderful oil painting he called "Grump." (pictured left) A third reward. My irreligious mother always said the 11th commandment was to "Reward Thyself." Thanks, Mom.

Yes, this was a good stop. We didn't get back on the road the next day until noon after checking out the town jail that Joachim had bought for another song and planned to fix up into an artist retreat and museum. Joachim thinks big, and I have no doubt he will accomplish his dreams. On a more mundane note, he told us as we were walking along the very quiet Mississippi that Mark Twain's birthplace is a very popular destination for Japanese tourists. Huh, right? I'm going to have to figure out that connection one day.

This was the hardest day of driving. The mileage wasn't quite as long as the Georgetown to Colby leg, but it was close, and we were almost at the end. Adrenaline stores were low. Despite, or because of, the excellent short stay with my friends, we had lost some of our travelling energy, and I knew we needed to be careful. On Mount Everest, they say most accidents and deaths occur on the descent. Everyone uses all their energy to get to the top and forgets the descent can be just as treacherous. We kept it together pretty well, though. The worst mistake I made was that I tried to put kerosene in the car instead of gasoline at a gas station in Kentucky. Thank God the nozzle didn't fit. The check engine light was off for the time being, though, and we were getting better gas mileage. I must have scared it into hiding.

After a fast food dinner at Wendy's in Louisville, Kentucky we pushed on to Huntington, West Virginia to a motel we found thanks to Stacey's iPhone. (This is not a plug – we are receiving no money from Apple; it was just a very handy tool. Kind of like a third person.) Arrival time? 11pm on the dot. There was a nice jolly clerk there to greet us. I think he gave us the AARP rate. We looked that bad.

The next morning, we pushed the six hours home and it was over. Or so I thought.

At John and Stacey's house, tired but happy.
The end....

Chapter 26 – Re-Entry

Stacey and I talked a lot over the next few weeks. It was our way of keeping the trip alive; it was very hard to let go and even harder to find enough people to listen to what we went through. People had their own lives to talk about. Even though I was happy to be home with my dogs and my husband, a large part of me was in Colorado and a smaller part of me was still on the road. To paraphrase the law of inertia – if your body has been in constant motion for five days, your mind will keep moving for ten days. Or something like that.

Here's what I wrote in Sadie and Sasha's blog to sum up the 16 Legs trip in 16 lines:

1) This trip would have been much harder without Stacey's iPhone.

2) This trip would have been much harder without Stacey. The driving would have been fine, but wrangling three dogs and two crates in and out of motel rooms on my own might have been nigh impossible.

3) McDonald's egg biscuits rock (in every state!).

4) Driving in the dark in Kansas is nice. The roads are straight.

5) Sasha's smile looks like her ugly face which looks like a sneeze.

6) You can get attached to a dog very quickly.

7) Going from 16 to four legs was incredibly hard.

8) Even when you don't look or act like a lady, men at a truck stop in Kansas will hold the door for you.

9) It is uphill to Colorado.

10) Always buy what catches your attention at the Colorado

Gifts truck stop.

11) Kansas is not as flat as I thought.

12) Beer tastes really good after you check into a motel at midnight.

13) The Mississippi River just looks like it has stories to tell.

14) Driving 3,400 miles is easier than real life.

15) Don't feed dogs breakfast before they get in the car; but make up for it with yummy dinners.

16) I'd do it again in a heartbeat.

Now Rob and I waited and watched to see if they would get adopted. First, they had to be judged as suitable for adoption. They had to get over that hurdle. I don't pray, but I spent a lot of time hoping, which I guess is essentially the same thing. It was so hard to come home and wait. We managed to totally avoid all the chores of Christmas by explaining "Laura drove three pit bulls to Colorado. Sorry, didn't have time to send a card."

And thanks to the Internet, we could keep track of the girls and Pooch. Every day I was on the website. If I missed a day, Rob checked. But there was nothing, no sign of them on the "Available for Adoption" page for weeks. That made sense, because dogs in the Behavior Program weren't available for adoption until they "graduated." But I wanted them to graduate quickly. My anxiety mounted because we were helpless and I was forgetting how hard it had become to manage a house with four dogs with strong personalities and divergent needs. I thought maybe we should have kept them. That thought kept growing until it threatened to take over all.

Finally, Sadie and Sasha's photos were up on the website along with very cute descriptions. Pooch took a while to be available for adoption; his issues came to light once he was back in a kennel environment. But in a few more weeks, his photo was up. It was also very cute. (The importance of the ability of good photography to "sell" shelter dogs simply cannot be overstated.) So they were all in the system. *This* was the "Mission Accomplished" moment.

I needed a new, manageable mission, so I made myself go back to the shelter and start walking dogs again. It was like dating again after a break-up. It felt weird, but soon I was back to falling in love at the drop of a hat with some shy, weirdo pit bull-ish looking dog. It amazed me how often the feeling was mutual, how willing the dogs were to trust me, or any human. The way most dogs respond to a stranger bursting into their space, grabbing their collar and taking them somewhere unknown, still moves me. Often I am so busy trying to walk as many dogs as I can, I forget the true magic of this moment. It is especially amazing when dogs who have just arrived after being picked up from the streets - or dropped off from a home that no longer works for them - trust you. They assume something good – or at least not bad – is going to happen. Not the shy ones like Sadie and Sasha, but most dogs, even the big scary looking ones. Even the ones that pull and act crazy and try and bite the leash and want to go after squirrels and you have to tell them no. They listen and let you restrain them even though they could easily kill you. It is an amazing testament to the nature of dogs and what it means to be domesticated. We should never, ever abuse that trust. No person will give that to you. No cat, for all their glory, will give that to you. My understanding is that horses will give that to you, but they do not curl up at your feet. Think about it. An animal you don't know lets you be in control. It's like a child getting into a stranger's car. Horrifying thought, right? But that is what these dogs are doing.

So, I kept walking dogs, and we kept checking the website obsessively. Sasha got adopted first, then Sadie then Pooch. Yea! By March, all had homes. Eleven months from when Rob and I started our fostering journey, we could breathe a sigh of relief. Our mission was finally, truly accomplished, almost exactly one year later. It was a strange feeling, though. Yes, it was mostly one of relief and joy, but there were veins of sadness and loss, too. Every success holds a kernel of death in it. Your striving, your hoping is over. That deserves to be mourned, even though you got everything you were dreaming of.

Chapter 27 – Sasha's Crisis and New Beginning

"We are going to have to drive back and **get her.**"

About a month later, towards the end of March, we found out that Sasha was returned to Longmont. This was not the plan. Rob is convinced we have to drive back and get her. (I told you I married a great guy, right?) Instead, we watched and waited. She still had a cute photo, she was still available for adoption. She was not on death row. This is not a crisis. This happens all the time. But not again to poor Sasha. How many times can one dog go through this?

The next week, I was back at the CASPCA, walking a shy pit bull mix who was available for adoption, but still wary. I was feeding her treats every time she walked by something that made her nervous so she would learn to associate things she initially feared with treats and then eventually replace her fear with indifference. I saw Ashley, the Front Desk Manager, and headed to see her. "Hey, how's it going?" I said. Sometimes going about your business and ignoring a shy dog for a bit works well, too.

"Oh, I'm so glad to see you. We just got a phone call, and apparently Sasha has been transferred to another shelter or something." (Ashley sometimes has issues with details, a fact I completely forgot as I panicked.)

"Seriously?" My head was spinning. Nooooooh. "Wait, we paid them $500 to take her. They can't do this," I said. It didn't make sense. This was the one thing that wasn't going to happen. She couldn't be where I couldn't get to her. What shelter? Is she okay? We were going to have to go back and get her, I thought.

"I didn't take the call," Ashley said sensing I was about to have a melt-down. "Let me get more details and I'll call you tonight"

"Okay…." I wasn't too sure what the details would be, but I didn't think they'd be good. I took my sweet, shy dog back to her kennel and went home. I walked Piper and Blue in such a state of anxiety that they felt it and walked on eggshells. When I got back, I had a message on my phone.

"Hey Laura, it's Ashley. I've got good news. It turns out Sasha was adopted, and the lady who adopted her just wanted to see if she could get some more background on Sasha. Here is her number. Will you call me after you've talked to her? Thanks. Bye."

Yes, this was good news, but not great news. Why did Sasha' adopter want more background? That meant there were issues. I held my breath and called the number. I don't even remember the details of the conversation, other than I spent the time explaining that Sasha did everything she was doing in the new adopter's house in our house as well. I talked and talked and talked, as if words would fix everything. Apparently, that helped, because I got this email the next day:

Dear Laura,

Thank you so much for calling last night. I really appreciate your sharing so much background information about Sasha and being so supportive. It's wonderful what you did for Sasha and Sadie to give them a chance to be adopted. And my husband and I can truly appreciate how lucky she, and

Sadie and Pooch were that you gave them yet another chance to be adopted in Longmont.

I'll be happy to update you more about life with Sasha. We're really enjoying your blog! It's so interesting to see Sasha interacting with the other dogs. And I can understand why they all must love your backyard.

Thanks again,

Marty

Sasha in her new home with Jerry.

It's going to be okay, I realized. No one sends an email like that if they aren't going to keep her, if they aren't already in love with her. It's going to be okay!

And then this came on Mother's Day, a month later:

Hi Laura,

I've been intending to write for a long time, and I really wanted to send pictures for Mother's Day. Sasha is doing very well though we are having issues with me being her "person." The pictures seem to tell a different story don't they? Actually that was a big moment to see her get up on the couch with Jerry. She had a hard time for quite awhile just getting used to going on walks alone with him. We met with the training program coordinator at Longmont Humane Society a few days ago and that was very helpful.

It was just recently that Sasha broke the "No Sasha On The Furniture" rule. She just wormed her way up! She knows that those are her special places now. On account of our felines we thought it wouldn't work out to let her do that. Left to right in the picture are Henry, a glimpse of Zachary's black fur in the windowsill, Piper and Harry.

The cats, with the exception of Zachary, have given Sasha a lot of "direction. "Wary" Harry has by far been the most outspoken in that regard. They've gradually eased up on her more knowing that she is not allowed to eat in the kitchen

with them or sleep in the master bedroom at bedtime. They're funny when Sasha gets in her "nuts" mode and tears around the family room tossing toys and whatever else of hers (including her bed) in the air along the way. They all scatter but they stay close by enough to watch her.

Sasha has been going to daycare two or three days a week for several weeks now and she just – Surprise –loves the other dogs! One of the staff there noticed Sasha's shy smile early on. She goes on pack walks too as part of her daily routine there. Sasha started Basic Dog Obedience class at the Humane Society three weeks ago. Coincidentally the owner of Uptown Dog where she goes for daycare is also teaching the class. Sasha is enjoying the experience.

I have to go now but I'll keep in touch. Hope all is well with you. Just the other day I was looking at your blog again about Sadie and Sasha because it's such a compelling story.

Sincerely,

Marty

Whew! And keep in touch she did, occasionally sending me Happy Mother's Day wishes on Sasha's behalf. The latest update from Jerry confirms that all is well, although Sasha still has her quirks intact:

We wish that she was more accepting of strangers. She's just fearful and barks (when someone comes to the door or when she hears a doorbell on TV) but is never aggressive. She is very attached to Marty and vies for her attention with Harry the cat. We still have two other cats as well.

Marty and her husband adopted Sasha thanks to exposure to pit bulls through their daughter. They kind of just wanted to do their part. And clearly, their hearts were big enough to take on an extra-large part. They took – and kept – Sasha, warts and all, thanks in part to their willingness to sue the resources that Longmont provided for adopters. I love them for helping Sasha and for helping me.

Lucky, sleepy Sasha is home. Finally.

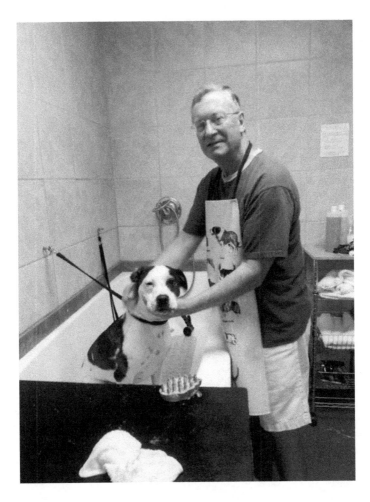

Jerry giving Sasha a bath. Love her expression.

Saving Sadie and Sasha

Chapter 28 - Pooch and Sadie, Also Happily Ever After

Sadie went quickly. Sadie was nutty in her own way, but she didn't have as many quirks or that "look" that Sasha did. The kind of look you had to look past, or into, depending on your point of view. I just wasn't as worried about her. Sadie was renamed Stella because there was already a Sadie at Longmont (an entire book could be written on the challenges of naming 5,000 shelter animals a year.) Here's the email I got from Sadie's new mom that made me cry and beam with joy at the same time. I love her too.

Hi Laura,

My name is Cody and I'm the lucky owner of Stella! She has come incredibly far since we adopted her in January! She comes to work with my boyfriend or I every day! She's got loads of play buddies and is a bundle of joy! Thanks for transporting her safely!

Cheers,

Cody Rose

Sadie, now Stella, and her new mom.

The best thing I realized is that Sadie and Sasha now had much better lives than they would have had living with me in our basement while I was anxious all the time. Sadie / Stella even got to appear in an advertisement at the shoe company where Cody works. She goes to work with her her every day and sleeps under her desk. What a life, right?

Sadie, now Stella, with her new dog park buddy, Santiago.

It took Pooch four months for his people to find him. But boy oh boy, did he find the right people. He got adopted and renamed Malcolm after Captain Malcolm Reynolds, a fictional character in a sci-fi television series. Pooch got a promotion! And he got to live with another pit bull mix and three cats. I was interested in how Pooch / Malcolm handled the adjustment since he took the longest to "graduate" from the behavior program. I called Chrysta, Pooch's new mom, and she was more than happy to talk.

"We were looking to adopt a pit bull or a pit bull mix, but had to find one who was cat friendly," she explained. Chrysta said they had seen his picture and bio on the Longmont website and drove with Maggie to see him from their home 40 miles away.

"We took him for a walk, leaving Maggie in the car, and then along with a behavior specialist from Longmont got the dogs together in an open play area. Since he was listed as 'dog selective' we wanted to make sure they got along." (Note – dog selective means, in my opinion, that they have sense. Not every dog likes every other dog, just like not every person likes every other person.)

"Maggie was a bit wary, but the behavior specialist said her signals seemed appropriate and that Malcolm responded to those." So Pooch / Malcom had a new family.

That seems like a real leap of faith, right? I asked Chrysta why she was willing to take that jump. She explained they had lost their second dog, a big, goofy, wonderful pit bull several weeks before and that Maggie was miserable. She wasn't eating and just slept all the time. They couldn't stand her pain and hoped a new dog would help. "We hadn't planned on doing it so soon. And the first two weeks were a little rough. There were a lot of disagreements between the two dogs. We weren't 100% sure it was going to work out."

Yup. Been there, I thought.

"But then they figured out their hierarchy, and Malcolm came out on top." Apparently Maggie used to be top dog, but she was okay with her new position. "It did take her out of her funk," Chrysta said.

"When we brought him home, he was very careful. He seemed wary and like he lacked confidence. We tried to get him up on the couch or the bed and he was reluctant. Now, of course, he's right up in our laps."

They had a similar difficult beginning with Maggie, but it lasted even longer. I asked her why she stuck it out with Maggie and Malcolm. I loved her response:

"I feel every animal and every person deserves a chance. A lot of people don't take the effort to understand animals. I wanted to give Maggie the chance to be the best dog she could be. As a society, we have created this situation with companion animals, and we don't follow through. It's our fault, and I feel a social responsibility to do something. When it doesn't exactly work out the way we want, we treat them as disposable, and they aren't."

Pooch, now Malcom. Above and in previous photograph. Happiness.

I could not have put it better myself. That's the thing about difficult dogs; they are like a secret handshake or password to a special club. And the other people in that club are super cool. I love Pooch's new family too.

Chrysta left me with this last nugget: "He does very well in the car. He really chills out in the car." Ha! That's my boy. Well, not mine, but you know what I mean. I was beaming when she said that.

It meant, to me, that we had given him a good experience in those 1,700 miles.

Chapter 29 - What Was it Like There?

So now that I knew where everyone ended up, I wanted to know more about what actually happened with them at Longmont. I needed to fill in the blank spaces.

"Sadie and Sasha were pretty withdrawn when they arrived," Moriarty told me. I winced. Apparently they also had some issues with each other in their new environment. "We put them together to ease the transition, but they had a fight," she said. "They fed off each other's negative energy, and they were still otherwise completely shut down in the loud, chaotic shelter environment."

I've never had a sister, but I can totally see it:

"It's your fault we're back here."

"Not mine, sister, it had to be something you did."

Moriaty said they split them up and "roomed them with other balanced, social, outgoing dogs. We like to separate siblings or dogs who come in together anyway to see if they can form new relationships."

"They started out in play groups sitting in the corner and were pretty happy to see each other. Sasha started out chasing other dogs off, then she would interact and Sadie would follow. The other dogs pried them out of themselves. And they would always investigate the play group handler," Moriarty added.

That made sense to me, like kids wanting to be the teacher's pet. At least they had learned that people were okay. So they became more comfortable, never super outgoing or playful, but dogs have different personalities just like people. Heck, watch an elementary school playground.

I learned about Sasha's first family that didn't work out. They had her for six weeks. "That family had other dogs – dacshunds – and reported that Sasha would be snarky with them." Supposedly Sahsa also developed house training issues – which Moriarty thought were stress related since Sasha was supposed to live outside. Clearly, that home was not a good fit. That made seven homes for one little girl not yet two years old. But apparently she was just biding her time until her saviors showed up.

"Every dog should have adopters like Sasha," Moriarty said of the her final family. "They do playgroups and classes with her. They are just committed to making it work and that's what it takes sometimes. Sasha is going to daycare and really coming out of her shell." Longmont puts a lot of resources into adoption follow-up, kind of like post-marriage counseling instead of pre-marriage counseling. I think these services helped give Marty and her husband the confidnece necessary to keep a dog with issues like Sasha.

Pooch was in the behavior department for 24 days, and in the shelter for a total of 86 days, almost 3 months. "Pooch was a completely different case," Moriarty said. " He was high energy, easily aroused and had some dog-to-dog issues. He showed some concerning behavior toward other dogs. He was easily frustrated."

That was so odd to me, although I guess I saw it before I loaded him in Charlottesville. On the trip, he was so perfect and deferential to Sasha. It goes to show that a dog's behavior is very environment based. And come to think of it, so is mine. And probably many people's.

"But we knew we had the well-socialized, stable dogs who could help him. Dogs can teach other dogs much more effectively and quickly than humans can. Our job is to supervise them. I can't teach a dog how to be appropriate. I can correct them, but other dog's corretions are much more appropriate," Moriarty said.

I asked Moriarty how she handled the intense nature of her work. "It is stressful work. Some days I am better at it than others. I have to leave work at work. Euthanasia decisions tear me up inside. I keep in mind success stories like Pooch and Sadie and Sasha," says Moriarty.

Mission. Freaking. Accomplished.

Saving Sadie and Sasha

PART FIVE: All In

Chapter 30- More Training for Me

The most amazing opportunity fell into my lap about a year after the Big Road Trip. If I learned anything from that experience, it's when to say yes to something crazy that I have absolutely no time or money for, but which feels totally right. It is those things that end up being life changing. I found out through Susanne, my former boss at the CASPCA, that THE Aimee Sadler would be giving a three-day shelter dog playgroup workshop in Roanoke, only two and a half hours from my home. I signed up right away. Even though the workshop – which was free thanks to the financial support of Animal Farm Foundation – was already full, the organizer was someone I knew. Well, we had never technically met, but thanks to a video I did for an ignored, older pit bull named Stella, he drove to our Charlottesville shelter and adopted her. He credits me for showing how great Stella was in that video. So from that bond, I was in. Now I would get to see with my own eyes behind the curtain of how dogs can be rehabilitated by other dogs.

The workshop was devoted to teaching us – shelter workers and volunteers – how to start and run playgroups. Sadler gave the group of about 40 a power point presentation at the beginning of the workshop. It was excellent, with lots of videos to illustrate her points. Then we went to the first shelter, a rural one near Roanoke, Virginia. Standing in a large, fenced in area, Sadler asked the staff to bring her the happy, easy, social dogs first so she could create a pack and then introduce the dogs that had been labeled "dog aggressive" later. (She's not crazy; she muzzles dogs she doesn't trust, which actually weren't that many.)

I was nervous. I am good at being nervous. I have oodles of practice. I was so trained by our policies at the CASPCA to keep dogs, especially pit bulls, apart lest anything bad happen. I understood intellectually that play groups were important but that was different than watching one with my own eyes. But it was beautiful, seeing twenty dogs romp around. Sure, there were the occasional tussles, and we did get to see one true dog-aggressive dog chasing full bore after another dog despite having a muzzle on. But mostly we saw dogs who were labeled as having problems with other dogs proving their labels wrong and having a blast with other dogs. Pit bulls, hounds, little dogs, big dogs, and three legged dogs all mixed up together.

Now, it doesn't work like this at the local dog park, and don't expect it to. Sadler and her co-worker had everything they needed to break up fights should they occur, plus years of experience at watching dogs. Some dogs, she would evaluate at the gate and turn away. At the local dog park, you have a variety of owners with a variety of experience – and inexperience – levels. There is nothing wrong with dog parks for some dogs, it's just an uncontrolled environment.

Why are play groups the key for shelter dogs? "They give you the biggest bang for your buck," Sadler says. They let you see how a dog really behaves and keep you from labeling a dog as dog aggressive when aggressive behavior only occurs on leash or behind barriers or during a single behavior evaluation when a dog was maybe feeling scared or crappy. Plus, they give you the knowledge of which dogs are well-socialized and easy and can help more difficult dogs. Finally, they help the dog get rid of some pent up energy so he or she can more easily adjust to life in a kennel for the rest of the day. A win-win-win in Sadler's mind.

Aimee Sadler "supervising" a playgroup in Roanoke.

In the play yard, Sadler was a calm, confident presence, even with the migraine that hung around for all three days of the seminar. She trusts dogs enough to turn her back once she has evaluated them. Dogs don't like staring anyway, so her relaxed presence helps the dogs relax.

Watching Sadler handle "conversations" between dogs that were going south was fascinating. She never intervened too soon, and usually the dogs would figure it out and stop posturing. They were communicating to each other in ways we did not understand. When she did have to intervene, she would start with using her voice, but then would follow her own advice: "If your voice doesn't work, shut up." Sadler would move on to tools like a spray bottle of water and an air horn. The air horn would almost always get the dogs' attention.

What? No hysterical screaming? That's my wheelhouse! Well, that and belly rubs. So clearly, I need to expand my repertoire. Oh, and all that love I showered Sadie and Sasha with? That was not the best. Love is good, bonding is bad. "It's cruel to make a bond with a foster dog and then break it," Sadler explained. I thought back to Sadie and Sasha at Longmont jumping toward me at the door of their kennel and my heart ached so much I thought it had broken again. Or at least sprained itself.

Three wet and cold days later, I was a believer and my head was so stuffed with learning, I needed to get rid of some old baggage. I tossed algebra and geography and the handful of songs I had almost learned on the guitar. I could use Google for maps and I didn't plan to solve for X anytime soon and well, the guitar will have to get along without me. (There is no way I can teach you what Aimee taught me, so please don't think this measly chapter is a road map of how to make shelter dogs play groups, it's just my story. And there are seminars you can go to .....I would encourage you to go).

Another Roanoke playgroup with Aimee Sadler (not in picture).
Many of these dogs were previously considered unsafe to interact with
other dogs based on their leash or kennel behavior.

Here are the main lessons I took way from those three magical days. (I'm lucky I didn't end up with the big red pit bull Grimm, too, or King, a tall skinny goofy shepherd looking dog, or Trinity, the three-legged pit bull)

Lesson 1 – Don't make assumptions.

Lesson 2 – Try, then try again another day.

Lesson 3 – Don't intervene too soon.

Lesson 4 – Dogs can squabble and then make up, LIKE PEOPLE

Lesson 5 – Some dogs may have a permanent personality conflict – LIKE PEOPLE

Lesson 6 – Don't overreact.

Ah, but overreacting is right there in that wheelhouse of mine nestled down for the night with hysterical screaming. It was something I would have to work on.

After the seminar's conclusion, it was incredibly difficult to come back to real life. I told anyone who would listen that if Sadler started a cult, I would run off and join. She didn't just try and help the difficult ones, either; she watched out for the good ones. Sometimes the good ones got tired of teaching the disorderly dogs how to behave. A tried dog – like a tired person – is more likely to be a jerk.

Back at the CASPCA, I felt a responsibility to put what I learned into practice. First, because I wanted to do it, although I was certainly nervous. Second, I knew I'd lose my nerve if I didn't do it. I ran it by Jennifer, the Director of Operations. She gave me a tentative okay. Sadler had done a workshop a year earlier at the CASPCA, and while the staff supported the idea in theory, implementing it took resources they didn't have. It was up to me now.

Play groups are hard work, these are not your dogs, and bad things can happen, usually thanks to handler error. But I had my spray bottle and airhorn, and a new belief that risk is what it is all about. I was sold after my second time making mini- playgroups of two when this giant pit bull, labeled in-house as "kind of a mess," had just played so happily and energetically with two very different dogs. Walking him back to his kennel on his leash, his tongue hanging out, I could just hear him. "Oh my god, lady, that was awesome. Can we do it again?"

One of the best things about dogs is that they do not engage in deception. They cannot tell a lie. You shouldn't either when you are around dogs. It is neither safe nor helpful to try and fake too much with dogs. Dogs keep you in the present moment. Use that. On the days I know I am not at my best, I do less with the dogs. I learned that the hard way. You also always have to be willing to let the dogs show you what they want or need. I often would have a plan to put a couple of dogs together and I was so excited about that plan that I forgot to notice that it was 17 degrees outside and one of the dogs was shaking from the cold and probably not really in the mood to play. Being careful is not being cowardly.

Overall, I learned to make myself do things I wasn't good at in order to get better, but I also learned to be gentle with my limitations. Both were good lessons and both were lessons I would never have learned without Sadie and Sasha.

Saving Sadie and Sasha

Chapter 31 – It's Not All Happy Endings and That's Okay

Well, it is not okay, but it is a part of the deal. Back at the SPCA, Joey was one I couldn't save. Nobody could, and we had to accept it.

At the shelter, I develop favorites; I can't help it. It's the only way I can relate to the world, to narrow it down a bit. I like to spend more time with a few dogs who need me than less time with more dogs. Thankfully, there are people who go the other way. It takes all kinds to care for all the dogs.

Anyway. So there was Joey. A chocolate brown pit bull. He was really big, and he knew it. He wore his size with pride, just like a football player or a swimmer. He was gorgeous, too. The first few weeks that I was back walking dogs after my Sadie and Sasha road trip, he would launch himself at the kennel door and bark like he wanted to kill me. There was something in his eyes that said: "I don't really want to do this, but I am scared and don't know what else to do." Or at least that is what I thought they said. So, I came back one day with hot dogs. After saying "No" and standing my ground when he came at me instead of flinching like a little kid, Joey stopped in his tracks. Then I squatted down with my body sideways to his and offered him a piece of hot dog. He took it gently. Then I asked him to sit, which he did quite promptly. This dog was trained. A few more hot dogs and he was wagging his tail. Magic! I did it! I fixed him! Ta Da!

Well, no, not really. But for a few days I thought I did. I brought him some more special food the next visit, and he happily wagged his tail. Then the third time, he lunged at me barking and growling. Unpredictable, that's what he was. He looked as confused as I did. He was this way with several of the staff, too. It would seem he was "fixed," and then he would regress. Of course, the kennel was no place for lessons to take hold, but thanks to the judicial process, we had no options.

You see, Joey was at the CASPCA on a court order, and he couldn't even be walked thanks to the law regarding court case dogs. (A dangerous dog case was proceeding against his owners.) I was still feeling pretty good about myself and Joey's potential until I talked to Ashley. Apparently the owner won her case and was going to get Joey back. He won't have to be euthanized. Yea! Then Ashley explained to me she is a "meth head" who lets the dog run free. By virtue of the court decision on the dangerous dog case, she could only have him back if she built a fence. In addition to a fence, she had to promise not to let him run free to be in compliance with the order allowing her to have the dog back. How can you count on a meth head to make that happen consistently? And what if I were walking my dogs by Joey's house and he ran out and attacked my dogs? I was frightened to think of a dog like that running free. Shoot, my dogs shouldn't run free; I don't know what they would do.

It is so complicated. Dogs live in our communities. It's easy to love a dog in a shelter. It's harder when it's messy and impacts your life and your dogs and their safety. It's all context. I was very sad when I went home.

Joey did eventually get euthanized. He was unpredictable with more people than just me, one of the big three reasons that will get a dog euthanized almost anywhere, even at Longmont. And his meth head owner couldn't create a safe enough environment for him to meet the court's demands. I still think about Joey, though and the circumstances of his life that sentenced him to death. Even more, though, I think about how a dog would have felt in a fight with a dog like that. These are the hard decisions that shelter workers and volunteers have to live with. They are few and far between, but you do not forget them. Joey would have been fine with the perfect owner. Maybe. Reality sucks, but it is all we have.

Saving Sadie and Sasha

Chapter 32 – Following in Footsteps

Two years later, I went back to work for the CASPCA for a while and brought home a new foster dog or puppy every couple of months. Here are pictures and a few words about those who shared our home recently. They will never know how much they owe to Sadie and Sasha.

Charlotte was skin and bones when an Animal Control officer brought her into the shelter. It turned out she had advanced Addison's disease. Rob and I brought her home as a hospice foster and loved her until she died, despite treatment, two weeks later. She was happy and warm here.

Hiccup also came to us in sorry shape. He was a solo puppy, allegedly found as a stray, about seven weeks old. In a few days, he blossomed into a ball of energy. But, amazingly, he would sleep through the night almost from the beginning. It was hard to let him go, but his adopters were friends of ours so we get to see him every now and then.

Rage was adopted from the CASPCA and then returned a day later for "exhibiting rage syndrome at 10pm." What? Staff and volunteers tried to rile up Rage (not her name, but how could we not call her that?) and never saw anything other than a sweet, normal puppy. But our Behavior Coordinator was still concerned because none of us had seen her behavior at the magical hour of 10pm. "Oh, give her to me," I said. Rob and I spent the evening playing with her – even staying up until 11pm! – and she never showed us anything other than normal puppy behavior. In fact, Piper even liked her. I brought her back the next day and declared her completely adoptable and she was adopted the next day. I actually met her again as an adult and she turned into a lovely dog.

Hank (pictured with Blue) came to us with a broken leg. After his surgery, he needed cage rest. But eventually, he needed a foster home, so I volunteered, because, well, look at that face. He was adorable, but we soon learned that keeping a puppy quiet while his leg is healing is impossible at our house. I had to bring him back to the vet at the CASPCA a couple of times to make sure his leaping off the furniture after Blue didn't damage his leg. Couldn't turn your back for a minute. He was adopted by a great guy.

Chalkie (left) and Tater Tot (right) were born in the shelter to a beautiful, sweet gray pit bull who came in very, very pregnant. Their real names were Amethyst and Jasper. They only needed to stay with us for a few days, but they were a lot of fun in that short time. A lot of mess, too, but that's what puppies do: eat and poop. They were quickly adopted by very nice families.

Bramble just stayed with us for a night. It was an experiment, like the one with Rage, and he also passed with flying colors. He was quite a handful in the shelter – very prey-drive and a "door darter" as well as a fence fighter. But he was young and probably had never been around caring humans or dogs who were not looking for trouble. I needed to give him a chance. He relaxed at home and was my favorite. I still miss him. He was accepted into Southampton Animal Shelter's behavior program in New York. (Of course, I drove him up there.)

Polly (nicknamed Lil P by Rob and me and called Stella by her new owners) had kennel cough and a bum leg when she came to the CASPCA. Her sister had also just died on the operating table. She needed a week of healing, so I scooped her up and brought her home. She spent a week sneezing, adorably, all over everyone. Thanks to this photo, published on Facebook, her adopters fell in love with her, and she is ruling the roost with two canine siblings.

Saving Sadie and Sasha

Chapter 33 - Home

I have always struggled with the concept of home. I have never felt roots anywhere. About the only things that conjure memories of my childhood are black standard poodles, red clay and the smell of tobacco curing in the sun. But I don't long to return to North Carolina. I am not a child of the south or indeed of any place. I struggle to care about a city or a state or a region or a culture. Except places I have travelled to on vacation. For some reason, those are all awesome.

This lack has been a source of sadness and wanderlust for me. Surely there is a place where I would feel at home, and I have long fantasized about finding it.

But home is not a place. It is other living beings. It is a state of mind, or of soul. My home is my husband, and my pets. My home is portable. My home is love. Sadie and Sasha taught me that, and for that lesson I am forever in their debt. I will try and pay it forward by giving "homes" to as many animals and people as I can for as long or short a time as I can.

Sadie and Sasha also taught me that I care for the misunderstood, the "other." People, dogs, wild animals, and, yes, even places that are on the outside looking in. I am an advocate by nature. I like to fight for the little guy. If you fight, though, you will fail. You will win some battles and lose some, even with yourself. You will never be as strong as you want to be. I was always worried about failing Sadie and Sasha. I noticed that most when I re-read the manuscript for this book. But if you beat yourself up too much for failure, you won't try again. As another talented dog trainer friend, Deven Gaston, explained to me, you don't have to be perfect to do some good. Dogs don't know you've failed as often as you do.

So, home is where I can do some good, feel some love and have some dogs. I guess that is where a lot of people feel at home.

PHOTO CREDITS

All photographs in this book were taken by the author or used with permission.

The wonderful photographs on pages 155, 159, 160, 163, 164, 168, 170, 171 and 174 were taken by Stacey Evans of Stacey Evans Photography.

Video clips of Sadie and Sasha's first days in our foster home and on their road trip to Colorado can be found at: sadieandsasha.blogspot.com.

Saving Sadie and Sasha

ACKNOWLEDGEMENTS

While this book was just meant to be the story of my journey with two little dogs, so many people were involved in helping them and me – and there are so many great organizations out there dedicated to helping dogs like Sadie and Sasha – that I wanted to mention a few:

Animal Farm Foundation

Bad Rap and many other less famous but just as hard working pit bull rescues

Best Friends

Facebook pages – DINOS: Dogs in Need of Space is a favorite

All of these organizations have great websites and provide good, solid information about how to help dogs in need. If you like getting your knowledge in person, a good option is to just go to your local shelter and talk to the people. Not on a Saturday, though, for God's sake. Saturdays are crazy. If the people there are not open to educating you and building a relationship, try another option. Search the internet, look in your phone book, call dog trainers, and become fans of interesting pages on Facebook. Find your people and your dogs.

You don't have to foster only the weirdos, though. Or even just pit bulls, although I do highly recommend it, clearly. A foster home can help a dog recover from surgery or a medical condition like heartworm, and it can provide a quiet space for a pregnant mother to have her puppies. There is nothing to be afraid of but a little extra laundry. Fostering is like a reverse vacation, or one of those volunteering vacations where you vaccinate children in Ecuador or clear trash from playgrounds in Detroit, except you can do it without leaving your home. All it really takes is love and a willingness to work. Spring is good for that. So are the end-of-the-year holidays because you are home and the shelter's staff would like to be. Often a shelter can provide flea medicine and the dog's food. So all you need is love.

My mother-in-law used to say: "It's not worth doing if it's not worth crying over." Well, we did our share of crying over Sadie and Sasha. We also did our share of laughing until we couldn't breathe. I like using tears as a measuring stick, though. It makes sense, and to me, there is nothing more depressing that having nothing in your life that you feel passionate enough about to cry over. Sure, pain will follow, but you can't live in fear of that pain.

I hope Sadie and Sasha have inspired you to think more about the dogs in our world and to maybe bring a few of the nuttier ones into your life. It is easier to do when you don't already have dogs in your home with their own quirks and peccadillos, but it's not impossible even when you have a full house.

"I miss those little nutjobs," Rob still says whenever we talk about Sadie and Sasha. We certainly didn't plan on having our weekend fostering adventure turn into all that it did. But most of the best things in life seem to happen without, or in spite of, planning. Not that I would suggest everyone reading this book throw caution to the wind and head to their local shelter and ask for the most screwed-up dog there. But I know a few of you will do it. If you do, just remember:

1)   Keep them safe.

2)   Keep yourself as well fed and rested as possible.

3)   Enjoy the ride.

It is well worth it. As friend and fellow animal lover Foust says: "Shy dogs appreciate you so much. You become their safe place." Is there a higher goal than to be someone's safe place?

So many people give so much of themselves every day to the goal of helping shelter dogs find homes. I would never have had the opportunity to play what little part I did in the lives of Sadie and Sasha if not for a whole line of people who did their part. I thank all of them with all my heart. I am especially, ridiculously grateful to those wonderful families who welcomed Sadie and Sasha into their lives, especially Sasha's new owners, because Sasha, well, they know why. I know you didn't do it for me, but you have made me feel kindly toward the human race. Thank you.

Creating a book starts as a solo project and evolves into a group effort. Thanks also to everyone involved with getting this story into print, especially Kristen Long who contributed her valuable editing skills, and my publisher, Tidal Press. Any flaws, however, are mine alone.

Undoubtedly, some will read this book and disagree heartily with things I did or wrote. They may be right; I may be right. I don't know. But I do know we all care, and that is enough to make us one tribe. Dogs help people form the most amazing connections. I never realized this until recently. I thought loving dogs was just about loving dogs. But it really is about so much more.

Sadie and Sasha say goodnight.

CPSIA information can be obtained
at www.ICGtesting.com
Printed in the USA
BVHW041333120620
581225BV00004B/141